THE ULTIMATE KITCHEN CONSULTANT

A complete guide to cooking and entertaining.*

LORETTA D. DOTY

*Because you're no dummy!

For Mom

My best friend and role model

With love

"The Ultimate Kitchen Consultant," by Loretta D. Doty. ISBN 978-1-60264-083-2.

Published 2007 by Virtualbookworm.com Publishing Inc., P.O. Box 9949, College Station, TX 77842, US. ©2007, Loretta D. Doty. All rights reserved. No part of this publication may be reproduced, stored in a retrieval system, or transmitted in any form or by any means, electronic, mechanical, recording or otherwise, without the prior written permission of Loretta D. Doty.

Manufactured in the United States of America.

Acknowledgements

First and foremost, to my darling husband, Virgil, without whose love, patience, and support I could not have written this book.

To our daughters, Deanndra, Ida, Laura, and Melissa, hugs and kisses for their confidence in me and their continuing encouragement, and especially to Melissa for her invaluable assistance and contribution to my work.

My deepest thanks and love to all of you.

Table of Contents

Building Blocks	6
Equipment	9
Appliances	12
Table Settings	13
Herbs	17
Spices	25
Wine Connoisseur	30
Temperature & Measure Equivalents	35
Meal Planner	38
Food Storage & Safety	40
Grocery List	47
Cooking Vocabulary	58
Medical Terms	155

Introduction

The Ultimate Kitchen Consultant is the result of over thirty years of experience in the field of cooking and entertaining. * It is intended to educate, inform, and inspire anyone who ventures into the kitchen.

As with any area of study, the potential cook should familiarize themselves with the proper terms, techniques, and tools of the trade. This reference was written with you in mind and will help you on your way to becoming a proficient cook and host/hostess.

A solid foundation is the key to success in any field. *The Ultimate Kitchen Consultant* lays the groundwork with basic information for a smoothly run kitchen. Newcomers, as well as those familiar with cooking and entertaining will find this guide to be a reliable source of information and advice.

Cooking is a rewarding experience and your can depend on *The Ultimate Kitchen Consultant* to help you along the way. Enjoy your time in the kitchen with newfound confidence and independence and impress your friends with your entertaining know-how.

*The information contained in this book came from so many sources over the years, both verbal and written, that I would never be able to account for them. I never intended to publish my notes as they were for my own use. It was my daughter, Melissa, who began gathering and compiling my notes, and urging me to publish them along with any advice I had to offer.

Building Blocks

Building Blocks is geared toward those of you who are setting up your kitchen for the very first time. Let it guide you through the basics of stocking cupboards and start you on your way to becoming a well-organized and capable cook.

Once you stock your kitchen, which does take time and money, and develop a system for maintaining it, you will find that it is so much more convenient and less expensive than those daily trips to the grocery store. A fully stocked kitchen also allows you to focus your attention on those last minute items and final details when preparing a special dinner or entertaining guests.

Cooking shows make preparing dishes look so easy, and if you kitchen is well stocked and organized, it will be. With a little planning and forethought, even beginner cooks can prepare meals with ease. It is amazing what you can accomplish when you are prepared!

This section may also be used as a quick reference for those of you who have been cooking for years and already know your way around the kitchen.

Canned and Bottled Foods

beverages	cocoa mix, coffee, cold drink mixes, non-dairy creamer, assorted sodas, sugar substitute, tea, bottled water
condiments	ketchup, mayonnaise, mustard, sandwich spread
fish	anchovies, clams, crab, salmon, sardines, shrimp, tuna
flavorings	almond, lemon, favorite liqueurs, vanilla
fruit	apricots, fruit cocktail, mandarin oranges, peaches, pears, pie cherries
juices	apple and apple cider, clam, grapefruit, orange, lemon and lime (reconstituted), pineapple, tomato, vegetable
liquor	mixes and assorted drinks for entertaining
meats	chicken, corned beef, ham, pork, tuna, turkey
milk	evaporated, condensed, dry
soups	broth (beef and chicken), chicken noodle, clam chowder, creamed (broccoli, celery, chicken, and mushroom), tomato
oil	vegetable, olive, canola, non-stick spray
olives	black, Spanish (whole and stuffed with pimientos or almonds)
pickles	dill, gherkins, relish

spreads	honey, preserves, jam, jelly, peanut butter, corn and maple syrup, molasses
vegetables	carrots, corn, green beans, mushrooms, peas pimientos, prtatoes, tomatoes (paste, sauce, and whole), prepared spaghetti sauce
vinegar	apple cider, distilled, red and white wine
wine	Choose an assortment of wines for cooking and entertaining. See **Wine Connoisseur.**

Dry Goods

baking chocolate	bittersweet chocolate, cocoa powder, milk chocolate chips, semi-sweet chips, white chocolate chips
cereals	a variety of hot and cold cereals, barley
chips	cheese puffs, corn and potato chips, pretzels
cookies	butter, chocolate chip, macaroons, shortbread (these can be already made, mixes, or ready to bake frozen dough, vanilla wafers
crackers	club, croutons, graham, party assortment, rye salting, whole wheat
flour	all purpose, whole wheat, rice, cake and cookie mixes, corn meal
gelatin	cherry, lemon, lime, orange, plain, strawberry
herbs	basil, bay leaves, chives, dill, dry mustard, garlic powder, marjoram, diced onions, oregano, parsley, poppy seeds, rosemary, sage, tarragon, thyme
legumes	beans, lentils, split peas
miscellaneous	instant mashed potatoes and rice, mushrooms, Parmesan cheese, assorted pasta, rice (brown, enriched, and wild)
leavening	baking powder, baking soda, yeast
nuts	almonds, peanuts, pecans, walnuts
paper goods	aluminum foil, coffee filters, cupcake cups, freezer bags, napkins, paper cups, waxed paper
pudding	banana, butterscotch, chocolate, coconut, custard, lemon, pistachio, Tapioca, vanilla

sauces	bouquet, chili, picante, salad dressing (bottled and mixes), soy, steak, Tabasco, Worcestershire
seasonings	allspice, bouillon (beef and chicken), cayenne, celery seed, chili powder, cinnamon, cloves, curry, ginger, mace, meat tenderizer, nutmeg, paprika, pepper (black and white peppercorns, ground), salt (coarse, iodized, and sea salt)
sugar	granulated, cubes, brown, powdered, raw
shortening	lard, vegetable
thickeners	corn starch, arrowroot

Refrigerated and Frozen Foods

butter	salted and unsalted, margarine
cheese	cheddar, cottage cheese, cream cheese, mozzarella
eggs	fresh or liquid substitute
fish	fillets, breaded fillets, seafood
fruit	fresh fruits, frozen fruits
ice cream	vanilla and assorted flavors
meat	beef, lamb and pork cuts, ground meats, sandwich meats, sausage (links or patties)
milk	buttermilk, half and half, whole or 2% milk, whipping cream
poultry	whole chicken and chicken parts
sour cream	real or cultured
vegetables	fresh vegetables for salads, frozen vegetables
yogurt	plain and flavored

Equipment

Every profession, including cooking, has its specialized tools that make life so much more convenient, but this equipment does not necessarily have to be expensive to be of good quality. Prioritize and take your time when selecting your tools. Doing this will save you unnecessary expense and allow you to customize your kitchen to suit your needs. Eventually, you will have all of the equipment you need to work with.

The following is a list of basic cookware, bake ware, and small appliances that are essential to every good cook and extras that are a great addition to a smoothly run kitchen.

Basic Cookware

1	6 qt. Dutch over	1	1 ½ qt. saucepan
1	2 qt. saucepan	1	3 qt. saucepan
1	8" frying pan	1	10" frying pan
1	double boiler		
1	2 qt. steamer insert	1	12" griddle
1	chicken roaster	1	9" x 13" roasting pan
1	batter bowl	1	5 qt. colander
1	stove top teapot	5	8" to 10" diameter stainless steel mixing bowls

lids for all of the above (Glass is convenient for checking food without uncovering the pan.)

- Copper bottomed stainless steel pans conduct heat better than stainless steel alone, though most cooks prefer stainless steel pans because they provide uniform heat conduction and are durable. Copper pans need to be polished occasionally but they can be a charming addition to your kitchen decor. Also, if you are unable to buy a full set of pans, select the largest ones first. (A small amount of food can be prepared in a big pan.)

Additional Cookware

1	set of heat resistant glass pots and pans	2	9" x 13" roasting pans
1	set of good quality non-stick pots and pans	2	14" round pizza pans
1	14" wok with utensils	1	turkey roaster

Basic Bake Ware

1	9" x 13" oblong cake pan	1	9" x 9" cake pan
2	9" round cake pans	1	12 cup muffin pan
1	bundt cake pan	1	loaf pan
2	9" pie plates	1	cookie sheet

Additional Bake Ware

1	set of heat resistant glass baking pans		
2	9" x 13' oblong cake pans	1	9" x 9" cake pan
2	9" round cake pans	2	13" x 18" sheet cake pans
1	12 cup muffin pan	1	mini-muffin pan
2	bundt cake pans	2	9" pie plates
1	cookie sheet	1	set of silicone bake ware

Basic Equipment & Utensils

1   15" x 20" cutting board

1   set of knives:
    bread	(A long, straight bladed knife with a serrated edge.)
    chopping	(A long, wide, tapering knife.)
    filleting	(A medium to long, narrow-bladed knife.)
    paring	(A small knife.)
    steak knives (Small tapering knives with serrated edges.)

1   pair of kitchen scissors (Sturdy scissors, specifically made for use in the kitchen.)

1	knife sharpener	1	bottle opener
1	can opener	1	cheese grater
1	egg timer	1	fruit and vegetable peeler
1	ice cream scoop	1	juicer (non-electric)
1	pizza cutter	1	small rolling pin
1	set of measuring cups and spoons		

1   set each (small, medium, and large):
    wooden spoons, wire whisks, silicone spatulas

1   6 piece set of stainless steel cooking utensils:
    spoon, slotted spoon, 2 spatulas, and 1 ladle

1	set of skewers	1	8"diameter wire strainer, 3" and 8" mesh strainers
1	pair of metal tongs	1	vegetable brush

2   kitchen towel sets:
    towel, dish cloth potholders, oven mitt

1	pair rubber gloves	1	set of 4 canisters
1	cookie jar		

Additional Equipment & Utensils

1	12" x12" cutting board	1	8" x 15" cutting board
1	15" x 20" cutting board		

1 set each:
knives, wooden spoons, whisks, spatulas, stainless steel utensils, skewers

1	clam knife	1	grapefruit knife
1	oyster knife	1	apple corer
1	avocado slicer	1	cherry pitter
1	garlic press	1	herb mincer
1	pepper mill	1	large marble rolling pin
1	tomato slicer	1	zester

4 kitchen towel sets:
    dish towels, kitchen towels, dish cloths, pot holders, oven mitt

Appliances

When buying a small appliance for your kitchen, ask around or check with a consumer products company prior to purchase. There are many name brands and store brands available, but a label does not ensure quality. Some appliances are more dependable and longer lasting than others, regardless of their brand or price tag. Shop and compare.

Basic Appliances

blender
large slow cooker
microwave oven
toaster

coffee maker
hand mixer
small food processor
waffle maker

Additional Appliances

bread maker
slow cookers:
    small, medium, and large
ice cream maker
espresso machine
stand mixer
large food processor
Belgian waffle maker

coffee mill
deep fryers:
    small and large
electric juicer
large microwave oven
4 capacity egg poacher
5 slice toaster with wide slots

Table Settings

When you choose your table settings, you need to take into consideration the type of entertaining you are planning because they establish the atmosphere of the occasion. For instance, an informal meal or get together calls for a casual setting, while an elaborate party or a formal holiday dinner requires a more formal one.

The items listed in this section can be bought at a decent price. So, take your time and know what you are buying before stepping up to the cash register. Again, a higher price does not always indicate better quality. Beautiful place settings can be had at bargain prices.

Also, you need to decide what type of entertaining you will be doing for the most part. Doing this will help you to focus on the items that suit your lifestyle.

When considering your casual settings, think in terms of the long-run. Is it practical? Will it hold up over the years or will you have to be replacing it? What you save in replacements, your can spend on extras or formal pieces.

Fine china is always a wonderful option for formal ware, but it is a big investment especially when you are just starting out. there are a variety of dishes, flatware, and so forth that are much more affordable and look just as nice. Choose wisely.

Basic Settings

6	dinnerware sets:	dinner plate, salad plate, cereal bowl, dessert dish, cup, and saucer
6	flatware sets:	knife, dinner and salad forks, teaspoon, iced-tea spoon, and soup spoon
6	glassware sets:	six, eight, and twelve ounce tumblers
6	guest sets (optional):	wine glass and miscellaneous bar glasses
6	serving bowls:	various sizes with serving spoons
3	serving platters:	small, medium, and large

1	salad bowl with servers		1	salt and pepper shaker set
1	sugar bowl with spoon and creamer		1	butter dish with knife

1   vinyl or linen table cloth for everyday

1   linen table cloth with napkins, place mats, and runner for entertaining

Additional Settings

An elegant or casual service for twelve:
>dinner plate, salad plate, bread plate, soup bowl, dessert bowl, coffee cup, and saucer
>A charger plate is optional.

12	sets of glassware:	water goblet, wine glass, and champagne flute specialized glasses such as brandy sifters, margarita, and martini glasses, short and tall bar glasses, shot glasses, etc.
12	sets of flatware:	dinner knife, butter knife, dinner fork, salad fork, seafood fork, dessert fork, teaspoon, iced-tea spoon, and soup spoon
2	serving sets:	spoons, slotted spoons, forks, and pie servers
3	sets:	linen tablecloths and runners for entertaining and holidays Lace tablecloths are optional.
12	sets:	napkins, napkin rings, and place mats to match linens

- If you plan to host formal dinners an all-white linen set (tablecloth, runner, and napkins) and a set of elegant napkin rings should be included in or added to you choice of linens.

Setting the Table

The art of setting a table plays an important part in dining and entertaining. Like painting, it is a creative talent because you are essentially taking a blank canvas and turning it into a masterpiece. And, like all great masterpieces, your table should reflect your unique personality and individual taste.

Setting a table for casual dinners and parties is fairly simple, but no less creative than setting a formal one. You will need to select linens that suit the occasion and, while the use of place mats is optional, centerpieces such as fresh flower arrangements, floating candles, and/or holiday decorations should be included to set the mood. Also, the dinnerware, glassware, and flat ware should match as it helps to pull the table together.

After you have set the backdrop to you liking, select your place settings and do the following:

Place the dinner fork on the left-hand side of the plate and the salad fork to the left of it, then place the rolled or folded napkin to the right hand side of the plate.

Next, set the knife (cutting edge facing in toward the plate), either on top of the folded napkin or just to the right of it if it is rolled. Set the spoon to the right side of the knife. The water glass goes just above and to the right of the dinner plate and the coffee cup to the right of the glass. Now, that was easy!

Setting a formal table is somewhat more involved because you have to deal with more dishes, glassware, and flat ware, but the basics are still the same. You will need to decide on linens, centerpieces, and whether or not you will be using runners and/or smaller accent pieces along the length of the table. It may seem overwhelming at first, but knowing how to lay a proper table is essential if you are planning a formal affair and it will come easily with a little practice. So, have fun with it!

First, make sure that you have a complete set of dinnerware, glassware, and flat ware. It is important that they match so that you table appears clean and elegant.

The next step is to choose your linens. White is usually best because it makes an elegant statement and accentuates your dinnerware, glassware, and flat ware. Now, is also a good time to decide whether or not to use a runner, a lace cloth over your linen, or lace rather than linen.

After selecting the linens, pick a centerpiece that suits the mood you want to create, i.e., elegant, festive, or intimate. Whichever you decide on, always keep the centerpiece low enough for your guests to be able to see each other over the top of it as this encourages conversation. With an extra long table, you may want to use small accent pieces such as floating candles or delicate flower arrangements. Doing this creates a continuous line of flow and pulls the table together.

Before you set the table, make sure that you allow 24 inches of table length for each place setting. Another detail to consider is your left-handed guests. You may prefer to seat them at the left end of the table so that they will not be knocking elbows with the person next to them. This may be a bit difficult to plan ahead of time but it will make your guests feel more at ease.*

There is a standard method for setting a formal table and it is easy to follow if you remember that everything is placed so that it is used from the outside moving in toward the dinner plate.

First, set your largest plate, which is the dinner plate, in the center.** Place the salad bowl on the dinner plate and the soup bowl on top of it.

Then, starting on the right-hand side, place your dinner napkin either folded in half or rolled up in a napkin ring next to the plate. Make sure your napkins match your linens and set them about an inch away from the edge of the table.

Next, set the knife, cutting edge facing in toward the plate on the folded napkin or to the right of the napkin if it is rolled. Place the soupspoon to the right of the knife. If you are serving shellfish, the seafood fork is placed to the right of the soupspoon.

On the left-hand side, place the dinner fork next to the plate and the salad fork to the left of it. The coffee spoon (teaspoon) and the dessert fork are placed directly above the dinner plate with the fork above the spoon, lying from left to right and facing in opposite directions. Set the bread dish above and slightly to the left of the dinner plate and place the butter knife across it at a diagonal from right to left.

When setting the glassware, place the water glass above and slightly to the right of the dinner plate. Place the wineglass just above and to the left of the water glass and the champagne flute above and to the right of the water glass. Place the coffee cup and saucer directly to the right of the water glass.

The following diagram gives you a visual idea of the layout:

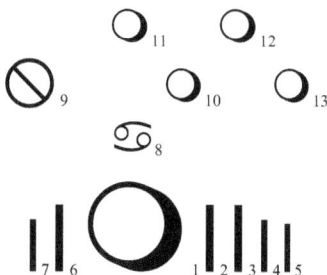

1. Charger plate, dinner plate, salad plate, and soup bowl; stacked that order.
2. Dinner napkin
3. Knife
4. Soup spoon
5. Seafood fork
6. Dinner fork
7. Salad fork
8. Coffee spoon (teaspoon), dessert fork
9. Bread plate
10. Water glass
11. Wineglass
12. Champagne flute
13. Coffee cup and saucer

* If you are following strict seating guidelines, then your left-handed guests will have to fall second to you guests of honor. The female guest of honor is traditionally seated to the right of the host and the male guest of honor is seated to the right of the hostess. As for the other guests, seat them according to compatibility in order to encourage conversation and create a pleasant, social atmosphere.

** A charger plate, which is a large plain or decorative plate, may be placed under the dinner plate. Leave this plate on the table throughout the meal as it helps keep your table linens from becoming stained and add a special touch to your place setting.

Herbs

Herbs are plants that are used in cooking because of the flavor and aroma they lend to foods. But without having this knowledge passed on to you, it takes many years of trial and error to figure out which herbs compliment which foods. The following information will save you the time and effort you would otherwise have to invest in deciding which herb to use.

The health benefits listed under each herb are based on personal education and experience. Herbs do contain elements that can react with the chemicals in prescription drugs and in over-the-counter medications. Their therapeutic uses are mentioned just as an FYI, not as medical advice. Please read the medical warning in **Medical Terms**.

anise
(Pimpinella anisum)

Aniseed. Anise, native to southern Europe and northern Africa, is a sweet smelling herb with fern-type leaves and a strong licorice flavor.
Anise is used in baking breads, cakes, and cookies. It is also used in the making of liqueurs. Anise comes in seed and extract form.

- Anise is an antispasmodic, expectorant, stimulant, and stomach tonic. It relieves the symptoms of colic and intestinal spasms. A hot cup of anise infusion is soothing and will help with insomnia. Cool anise tea will increase milk production in nursing mothers.

balm
(Melissa officinalis)

Lemon balm, native to Europe, is a member of the mint family with leaves that have a fresh, lemony scent.
Balm is rarely used in cooking.

- Balm makes a soothing tea and acts as a stomach tonic. It soothes the digestive system, relieves headaches, reduces menstrual cramps, and helps regulate menstrual cycles. Chewing balm will ease toothache pain, and a poultice may be applied to insect bites and scrapes.

basil
(Ocimum basilicum)

Sweet basil. Basil, native to Europe, is a member of the mint family and has a sweet, minty aroma.
Basil leaves are used in tomato dishes, vegetables, salads, French dressing, pizza, pasta, rice, stew; and in seafood and meat dishes. Basil comes in fresh and dried form.

- Basil is an antispasmodic and stimulant. It supports the gastrointestinal system reduces vomiting, and promotes menstruation. A cup of hot tea relieves headaches and an infusion works as a cough suppressant. A poultice may be applied to insect, cat, and dog bites.

bay leaves
(Laurus nobilis)

The bay tree is a European laurel and has leaves with a strong, bitter flavor.
Bay leaves are used in bouillon, chowder, soups, stews, marinades, spaghetti sauce; and in fish, meat, and poultry dishes. Use the whole bay leaf and remove before serving. Bay leaves come in fresh and dried form.

- Bay leaves are an astringent and a stomach tonic. Bay leaf tea helps the gastrointestinal system.

> Bay leaves are sometimes mistakenly called laurel leaves because they are members of the same family, but laurel leaves are poisonous!

caraway seed
(Carum carvi)

Caraway, native to Europe, is an aromatic biennial member of the parsley family. Like anise, caraway has a licorice flavor.

Caraway seed is used in cakes, cookies, sauerkraut, cabbage, soups, stews, chowders, cheeses, cheese spread, salad dressings, vegetables;fish, meat, and poultry dishes. Caraway gives rye bread its distinctive flavor, and is used to make kümmel and sometimes schnapps. Caraway comes in seed form.

> Caraway is used as an antispasmodic, expectorant, and stomach tonic. A cup of tea will increase appetite and help digestion. It also helps colic, menstrual cramps, and promotes the flow of milk in nursing mothers. An infusion of caraway may be used for rheumatism and eye infections. a poultice will ease toothaches and heal bruises.

cardamom
(Elettaria cardamomum

Cardamom, indigenous to southern India, is a member of the ginger family but also grows in other tropical regions. It has an aromatic capsular fruit but it is the seeds that are used as a spice and in medicine. Cardamom has a sweet, aromatic, pungent flavor.

Cardamom is the primary spice in Danish pastry. It is also used in fruit salads, fruit pies, gingerbread, sweet breads, cakes, coffee cake, cookies, puddings, and in pickling. Cardamom comes in both ground and whole seeds.

> Cardamom works as a stimulant and stomach tonic. It is used to increase appetite and help the gastrointestinal system.

celery
(Apium graveolens)

Celery or *smallage*, native to Europe, is a member of the carrot family. The celery leaves, stalks, and seeds are used in cooking.

The seeds are used primarily in pickling, soups, stews, potato salad, cheese, and pastry. They are also used in breads, dips, sandwich spreads, salad dressings, stuffings, and chicken rice.

Celery leaves and stalks are used in soups, stews, sauces, stuffings, poultry, roast, pot pie, and vegetable juice cocktail. Celery comes in fresh, dried, and seed forms.

> Celery is used as an appetizer, diuretic, sedative, stimulant, and stomach tonic. Celery juice increase appetite, helps with gastrointestinal problems and liver function, increases the flow of urine, and encourages menstruation. A seed decoction helps bronchitis, rheumatism, skin problems, and calms the nerves.
> Do not use celery therapeutically, if kidney problems are present.

chervil
(Anthriscus cereifolium

Chervil, native to Europe, is a delicate fern-like member of the parsley family. Though similar to parsley, it is more aromatic and has a sweeter flavor than parsley.

Chervil is used in soups, salads, in melted butter for fish sauce, and in egg and cheese dishes. Chervil comes in fresh and dried form.

- Chervil is used as a diuretic, expectorant, and stimulant. An infusion of chervil helps to lower blood pressure. Chervil juice relieves menstrual cramps and aids digestion. It may also be applied to abscesses and eczema.

chives
(Allium schoenoprasum)

The chive plant, native to Europe, is a member of the onion family. The grass like delicate leaves have a mild onion or garlic flavor and aroma. Chives are used as topping on baked potatoes, in soups, salads, vegetables, meats, poultry, fish, omelets, and egg dishes. They come in fresh or dried form.

- Chives are used to increase appetite and to promote digestion. Because they contain iron, chives may help in treating anemia. Chop the fresh leaves finely and serve them on a baked potato, salad, etc. May also be eaten alone.

dill
(Anethumas graveolens)

Dill is indigenous to Europe as well as to North and South America. Dill has a fresh, delicate flavor and aroma.
Dill is perfect in fish dishes and sauces. The leaves are also used in breads, pasta, rice, soups, salads, salad dressings, sauces, shellfish, and chicken. The seeds and stalks are used in making pickles and sauerkraut. Dill is available fresh, in dried leaves, and in seed form.

- Dill is used as an antispasmodic, carminative, diuretic, and for insomnia. A cup of hot tea will help an upset stomach. It will also encourage the flow of milk in nursing mothers.

fennel seed
(Foenuculum vulgare)

Fennel is a Mediterranean herb that also grows wild in Europe and the U.S. It is a member of the parsley family and has a very strong licorice flavor.
Fennel is used in breads, soups, seafood salads, salad dressings, marinades, pickles, sautéed mushrooms, and vegetables. It is especially good in fish dishes. Fennel comes in seed form.

- Fennel is an antispasmodic, diuretic, expectorant, and stomach tonic. It is an old remedy for digestive problems, especially colic. Whole or ground fennel seeds sprinkled on food will decrease stomach gas. Fennel tea also helps with jaundice, as an eyewash for irritated eyes, for insect bites, and food poisoning.

garlic
(Allium sativum)

Garlic, native to Europe, is a member of the lily family and has a flavor similar to an onion but its flavor is stronger and more pungent. Small individual bulbs, commonly referred to as cloves, grow together to form one large bulb and are enclosed in a white outer skin.
Garlic is used in virtually every entree and it is especially good in breads, soups, stews, salads, salad dressings, sauces, marinades; and in fish, poultry, meat, tomato, and vegetable dishes. Garlic comes in many forms but fresh garlic, or whole clove or minced garlic that comes in a jar and can be refrigerated are best. If these are not available, then the next best types are powdered or minced. Garlic salt is not recommended as it contains a lot of salt which makes it difficult to correct seasoning.

- ❀ Garlic works as an antispasmodic, diuretic, and expectorant. When eaten on a regular basis, garlic stimulates the digestive and the immune systems, regulates the liver and gallbladder, helps chronic bronchitis, lowers blood pressure and LDH cholesterol, counteracts arteriosclerosis, and combats intestinal infections and worms. A syrup made with crushed garlic cloves and honey works well as a cough syrup.
- ✎ The health benefits of garlic are too numerous to go into. Eat lots of garlic!

horseradish Horseradish, native to southwestern Europe and western Asia, is a member of the
(Armoracia mustard family and has a hot, spicy flavor.
lapathifolia) Horseradish is used primarily as a relish with roast beef, oysters, and tongue. It is also used in some spreads and sauces. It comes in fresh and relish form.

- ❀ Horseradish is a diuretic and stomach tonic. Take horseradish in small amounts with honey or sugar. It is used for urinary tract infections (UTI's), intestinal trouble, and sinus and lung problems. A poultice may be applied for rheumatism and to stimulate blood flow in hands or feet that have been over exposed to the cold.
- ✎ If diarrhea or night sweats occur, stop taking it.

juniper A juniper is an evergreen shrub from the cypress family which is widely found
(Juniperus in Europe and North America. Dried juniper berries have a pungent, slightly bitter
communis) flavor.
Juniper berries are used primarily in making marinades, game dishes, sauerkraut, and gin.

- ❀ Juniper berries are used as an antiseptic, a diuretic, a stomach and intestinal tonic for infections, inflammations, and cramps. It is also used to increase the appetite, to burn fat, and for UTI's. The berries may be brewed into a tea or eaten whole. As a disease preventative, gargle with a strong tea or chew a few berries after exposure to a contagious disease. A strong tea will kill mold and mildew if used as a disinfectant spray.
- ✎ Avoid altogether if nursing or pregnant. Ingesting large doses of juniper berries or taking them for an extended period of time can irritate the kidneys and urinary tract. People who are prone to UTI's or have kidney problems should use caution when taking juniper for health reasons.

marjoram Marjoram, native to the Mediterranean area and Asia, is a member of the mint
(Majorana family. Marjoram has a sweet, flowery, minty flavor with a touch of bitterness.
hortensis) Marjoram is used in breads, soups, salads, salad dressings, sauces, chowder, meat, game, poultry, fish, shellfish, vegetables, egg, and tomato dishes. It is especially good in lamb dishes, but do not use in sweet foods. It is available fresh, but also comes in dried whole and ground leaves.

- ❀ Marjoram is used as an antispasmodic, expectorant, and a stomach tonic. Marjoram tea alleviates headaches, coughs, and respiratory problems. It also eliminates stomach and intestinal cramping, and helps to regulate menstrual cycles. Marjoram makes a soothing tonic and relaxing bath concentrate.

onion
(Allium cepa)

Onions, indigenous to the mountains of North America and other mountainous areas around the world, belong to the lily family and have a hot, zesty edible bulb. Onions are a very versatile seasoning and are used in just about every savory dish. They come in several varieties and are available fresh, as a juice, and in dried form (chopped, minced, and flaked).

- Onions are used as an antiseptic, antispasmodic, diuretic, expectorant, and stomach tonic. Onion juice can be used to lower blood pressure and as an antiseptic to cleanse the intestinal tract. Raw onion relieves heartburn and gas pains, and a slice of onion or onion juice may be used to clean an infected wound. Onion juice mixed with honey makes a good cough syrup.

oregano
(Origanum vulgare)

Oregano or wild marjoram, indigenous to the mountains of North America, is a perennial from the mint family. It has a strong, aromatic flavor similar to sweet marjoram but is somewhat stronger. Wild oregano (*Monarda menthaefolia*), native to the Rocky Mountains, has the best flavor but is diffucult to find. The bright lavender flowers of this variety add superb flavor to any dish that calls for oregano, but are notable piquant and should be used sparingly.

Oregano is used in Southwestern U.S., Spanish, Greek, and Italian dishes. It is especially good in chili and tomato dishes, soups seafood salads, chicken, fish, lamb, pork, pasta sauces, pizza, and stuffing. Oregano is available fresh or in dried whole or ground leaves.

- Oregano leaves and flowers are used as an antispasmodic, expectorant, and stomach tonic. Sipping hot oregano tea or applying a hot tea compress to the throat, will alleviate a sore throat. A poultice applied to sprains and swelling will speed up recovery. A few drops of warm juice extract in the ear canal works well for an earache. A drop of oil will help a toothache.
- Like all members of the mint family, oregano is a source of carvacrol (a liquid phenol) which is used as an antiseptic, disinfectant, fungicide, and in perfumes.

parsley
(Petroselinum crispum)

Parsley, native to Europe, is a member of the carrot family with a spicy fragrance and pleasant flavor.

Fresh parsley is used as a garnish and in salads. It may be used in breads, salads, soups, sauces, stuffings, and in meat, poultry, and fish dishes. Parsley comes in fresh and in dried forms.

- Parsley is used as an antispasmodic, diuretic, and expectorant. Parsley tea is used for asthma, coughs, fever, jaundice, kidney stones, suppressed menstruation, and urinary problems. A poultice can be applied to swollen glands or breasts, or to dry up milk in nursing mothers. A tea made from the seed will kill head lice and fleas.
- Parsley is rich in potassium. Potassium builds resistance to cancer.

poppy seed
(Papaver somniferum)

Poppy plants, scattered world-wide, have bright red, violet, orange, or white flowers, and yield seeds that are blue in color. Poppy seeds are crunchy and have a nutty flavor.

Poppy seeds are used as garnish, on foods and baked goods. They are also used in breads, salads, fruit salads, salad dressings, cheeses, casseroles, and vegetables.

❋ Poppy seed has no value as a medicinal herb. The medicinal part of the poppy is the milky substance contained in the unripe capsules of the opium flower.

rosemary
(Fosmarinus officinalis)

The rosemary bush, native to Southern Europe and Western Asia, is a member of the mint family with leaves that resemble pine needles both in appearance and aroma. Rosemary leaves have a fresh, sweet flavor.

Rosemary is used in breads, soups, stews, salads, fruits, fruit juices, fish, seafood, meat, and vegetable dishes. It is excellent with lamb and pork. Sprinkle on charcoal when barbecuing for an appetizing aroma and flavor. Rosemary is available fresh and in whole or ground dried leaves.

❋ Rosemary is used as an antispasmodic, astringent, stimulant, and stomach tonic. Rosemary tea alleviates headaches, colds, colic, increases circulation, and helps raise blood pressure. Rosemary oil may be used for rheumatism, abrasions, sores, and eczema.

❧ Limit therapeutic intake of rosemary to occasional use and in small amounts. Rosemary is poisonous if taken too often and in large amounts!

Saffron
(Crocus sativus)

The saffron plant, native to the Mediterranean area, has reddish orange stigmas with a sweet, pleasant smell and flowery taste. The saffron stigmas are used in French, Mediterranean, Middle Eastern, Spanish, and South American cooking. Saffron is used in breads, soups, sauces, chicken, seafood, paella, arroz con pollo, bouillabaisse, risotto, rice, and cakes. It is available in dried form.

❋ Saffron is a diuretic and laxative. Saffron is an old and reliable remedy that works especially well for cold and flu symptoms. The tea is used for stomach and intestinal cramps, suppressed menstruation, and to alleviate the symptoms of scarlet fever. A poultice may be applied to relieve skin irritations.

sage
(Salvia officinalis)

Sage is native to Europe, but also grows wild in the Rocky Mountains. It is a member of the mint family and has big grayish-green leaves with a strong mint scent and slightly bitter flavor.

Traditionally, sage is used in sausage and in stuffings for turkey, goose, and duck. It is also good in soups, chowders, dressings, sauces, marinades, fish, poultry, beef, baked beans, lima beans, potatoes, tomatoes, cheeses and, especially, in pork and veal dishes. Sage is available fresh or in dried leaves, whole or ground.

❋ Sage is used as an antispasmodic, astringent, expectorant, and stomach tonic. Sage tea helps with night sweats but, taken in large quantities, it will induce sweating and help to lower fevers. It also aids the digestive system, makes a calming drink, helps tonsillitis, dries up the milk in nursing mothers, and decreases heavy menstrual flow. A sage poultice will help stop bleeding and heal injuries faster. Sage may be applied to insect bites.

❧ Limit therapeutic intake of sage to occasional use and to small amounts. Nursing mothers should not take sage as it will stop the flow of milk.
Do not confuse sage with the sagebrush plant that grows throughout the western U.S. Sagebrush is not an herb.

savory *(Satureja hortensis)*	Savory, sometimes called summer savory, is native to the Mediterranean region and is a member of the mint family. The leaves and flowers of this annual have a strong spicy, flowery aroma. Savory is used in soups, stews, stuffings, fish, poultry, meat, meatloaf, hamburger patties, and tomato dishes. It is great in all bean dishes, including peas and lentils. Savory is available in fresh and in ground forms. ❀ Savory is an astringent, expectorant, stimulant, and stomach tonic. Savory tea is used for stomach and intestinal cramps, nausea, diarrhea, indigestion, to increase appetite, and for sore throats. 🍃 Winter savory may be used interchangeably for its health benefits.
sesame seed *(Sesamum indicum)*	Sesame is a tropicla herb, native to East India, with seeds that have a nutty flavor. Roasted sesame seeds have a flavor that is similar to roasted almonds. Sesame seeds are sprinkled on breads, salads, soups, cookies, cakes, candy, and muffins. They are also used in making salad dressings, soup, stuffing, dips, cheese spread, and dumplings. ❀ The medicinal value of sesame seed is unknown. 🍃 Sesame oil comes from crushed sesame seeds and is used as food, in pharmaceuticals, and in cosmetics.
spearmint *(Mentha spicata)*	Spearmint, scattered world-wide, has stems and leaves with a fresh scent and a sweet, refreshing flavor. Spearmint is widely brewed into a refreshing tea. The fresh leaves are used as garnish for iced drinks, fruit salads, and almost all deserts. It is also used in lamb dishes, to make mint jelly, and in sauces. Mint extract is used in cakes, cookies, and candy. Mint is available fresh, dried, as an extract and an aromatic oil. ❀ Spearmint is a mild antispasmodic and diuretic. Because it is so gentle, spearmint will benefit even those who are very ill. It supports the gastrointestinal and urinary systems, and helps with stomach and intestinal cramps and UTI's. A hot cup of tea is relaxing and promotes a restful night's sleep. A cold glass of spearmint tea is calming and refreshing, and works for nausea. Pregnant women should avoid spearmint tea as it will induce labor. 🍃 Fresh leaves can be frozen in ice cubes for cold drinks. Spearmint should always be kept on hand and a pitcher of tea will stay fresh for up to a week in the refrigerator. Spearmint is healthy for young and old alike.
tarragon *(dracunculus vulgaris)*	Tarragon, native to Europe, is an aromatic herb with a flavor similar to anise. Tarragon is best in salads and turtle soup. It is also used in marinades, sauces, ragout, roast, fish, shellfish, poultry, egg dishes, and meats. Tarragon gives Béarnaise sauce its unique flavor and is used to make tarragon vinegar. It is available fresh and in dried leaves. ❀ Tarragon is used as a diuretic, sleep aid, and stomach tonic. Tarragon helps indigestion, stimulates urine production, and encourages the onset of menstruation. A hot cup of tea before bedtime will help with insomnia.

thyme
(Thymus vulgaris)

Thyme, native to Europe and Asia, is an aromatic member of the mint family with a pleasant peppery-mint scent and flavor.

Thyme is used in a bouquet garni, clam chowder, fish, poultry, meat, stuffing for fish and meats, tomato and cheese dishes, vegetables, and to flavor Benedictine liqueur. It is available fresh and in dried whole or ground leaves.

- ✺ Thyme is an antiseptic, antispasmodic, expectorant, sedative, and stomach tonic. It aids the gastrointestinal system, encourages menstruation, and has been used to get rid of intestinal worms. A hot cup of tea works for fevers by increasing perspiration and may be use to encourage sleep and reduce nightmares. A warm infusion helps with colds, sore throats, and tonsillitis. Thyme oil has been used in mouthwash and toothpaste because it is an antiseptic. A thyme compress may be used externally to increase circulation and for shingles.
- ✎ Use thyme in moderation. Symptoms of poisoning and over stimulation of the thyroid gland may result from overuse.

✺ Health benefits of a specific herb.
✎ Note or explanation.

Always steep herb teas.
Never boil.
Never use aluminum pots or pans to prepare tea.

Spices

Like herbs, spices are seasonings that are used in cooking because of the flavor and aroma they lend to foods. But, without having this knowledge passed on to you, it takes many years of trial and error to figure out which spices compliment which foods. The following information will save you the time and effort you would otherwise have to invest in deciding which spice to use.

The health benefits listed under each spice are based on personal education and experience. Certain spices do contain elements that can react with the chemicals in prescription drugs and in over-the-counter medications. Their therapeutic uses are mentioned just as an FYI, not as medical advice. Please read the medical warning in **Medical Terms**.

allspice
(*Pimenta officinalis*)

Pimento. Allspice is indigenous to the West Indies, and Central and South America. It is the aromatic berry of the pimento tree with a flavor comparable to a combination of cinnamon, cloves, and nutmeg.

The whole dried berries are used in beverages, soups, beef and fish dishes, and in pickling and preserves. Ground allspice is used in cakes, cookies, pie and cobbler fillings, French dressing, and in spaghetti sauce. Allspice is available in whole and ground form.

- Allspice is an aromatic, carminative, stimulant, and stomach tonic. Allspice tea makes a good mouthwash. Allspice oil is used for toothaches and makes a good ointment or poultice for arthritis, joint aches, and rheumatism. Allspice tea or oil may be used for indigestion or excess gas. It may also be used as a relaxing bath additive.

bouillon

Bouillon is a clear soup made from boiling beef, chicken, or fish. It is an excellent base for a variety of foods.

Bouillon is used in soups, stews, stuffing, chicken noodles, dumplings, pot pie, rice dishes, spaghetti sauce and in just about any beef, chicken, or fish dish.

- Bouillon has no medicinal value in and of itself but it does make a soothing broth. Taken hot, it is used for sore throats, colds, after tooth removal, and in other instances when solid foods are not tolerated well.

capers
(*Capparis spinosa*)

Capers, native to the Mediterranean region, are the unopened flower buds of the low growing prickly caper shrub.

These buds are pickled and used in sauces, with cabbage, eggplant, tomatoes, and other vegetables.

- Capers may be used to increase the appetite.

cayenne
(*Capsicum frutescens*)

Cayenne, native to the American tropics, is the pungent red powder made from the long twisted red peppers of a perennial pepper plant.

Cayenne pepper is used to add heat to a variety of dishes especially in Cajun cooking.

- Cayenne is an appetizer, digestive, irritant, and tonic. An infusion works for stomach or intestinal cramping. A sprinkle of cayenne powder will increase appetite and will shorten the duration of a cold. However, taking cayenne therapeutically over an extended period of time may cause gastroenteritis and kidney damage. A liniment may be applied to areas with arthritis, pleurisy, or rheumatism.

- Use with caution as prolonged or excessive use may cause blisters. Those with stomach ulcers or chronic gastrointestinal problems such as colitis or irritable bowl syndrome should avoid taking cayenne altogether. It may irritate ulcers and lead to internal bleeding.

celery seed
(Apium graveolens)

See celery under Herbs.

chili powder

Chili, indigenous to Mexico and Central America, is a plant that produces pods. These pods are dried, ground, and mixed with cumin, garlic, and oregano to create chili powder. It has a sweet, pungent flavor that ranges from mild to very hot. Chili powder is used to add heat to a variety of dishes and in Mexican/Southwestern U.S. cuisine including chili con carne, enchiladas, and tamales.

- Chili powder is not used as an herb, in and of itself, but may be sprinkled on food or used to make a chili stew. Chili stew, eaten alone or with other foods, is good for sore throats, colds, and will clear the sinuses.
- Do not confuse chili powder with the pure ground chili *(Capsicum annuum)* which is most often used in cooking and in medicine.

cinnamon
(Cinnamomum zeylanicum)

Cinnamon, native to Asia, is the aromatic inner bark of the cinnamon tree, an evergreen member of the laurel family.

Cinnamon is one of the most versatile spices. It is used in dessert dishes, cinnamon sugar, breads, cakes, cookies, stewed and dried fruit, fruit compote, fruit pie fillings, dessert sauces, preserves, beverages, French toast, doughnuts, cinnamon rolls, beef, pork, poultry and in pickling. It is sprinkled on cakes, cookies, pies, rice and tapioca puddings, and many other foods. Cinnamon is available in sticks and in ground form.

- Cinnamon is a stomach tonic and antiseptic. Cinnamon tea helps with nausea, vomiting, and diarrhea. The tea will stimulate digestion and relieve excess gas. A decoction of cinnamon will relieve flu symptoms and cinnamon oil helps with colds. Sprinkle some cinnamon in a hot drink for gastrointestinal and sinus problems, as well as for colds.

cloves
(Eugenia caryophyllat)

Cloves, native to the tropics, are the unopened, dried buds of the tropical evergreen clove tree and have a hot, sweet flavor. Cloves are used in sweet dishes, beverages, ham, tongue, pomander balls, breads, cakes, cookies, fruit pies, and gingerbread. They are available in whole or ground form.

- Cloves are used as an antiseptic and stomach tonic. Clove tea will relieve nausea and a few drops of clove oil in a cup of water will stop vomiting. Placing a drop or two of clove oil into a cavity and packing it with cotton will numb toothache pain. Chewing on a clove will freshen breath.

coriander
(*Coriandrum sativum*)

Coriander or cilantro (Spanish), native to Europe, is a member of the parsley family. Cilantro refers to the leaves and coriander to the seeds. Both the leaves and seeds have a spicy, lemony taste, though their flavors differ slightly.
Coriander seed is used in pickling spice and ground coriander is used in making candies, cookies, pastry, gingerbread, apple pie, applesauce, stewed fruit, soups, stew, fish, poultry, meat loaf, hamburgers, game, meat sauces, curry powder and curry sauces.
Cilantro is used in soups, stew, sauces, and in fish, poultry, and meat dishes. Cilantro is available in fresh and dried form. Coriander is available in seed and ground form.

- ❋ Coriander is used as an antispasmodic, appetizer, and stomach tonic. Coriander tea works well for gastrointestinal problems and aids the heart. A poultice may be applied externally for arthritis, rheumatism, and joint aches. Coriander improves the flavor of other herbs.

cumin
(*Cuminum cyminum*)

Cumin, native to the Far East, is an aromatic herb from the carrot family with a robust flavor. It is used primarily in Mexican/Southwestern U.S. cuisine, chili powder, and curry powder. It is also used in breads, cookies, beans, soup, stew, salad dressings, barbecue sauce, marinade for shish kebabs, cheese, game, rice, potatoes, and cabbage. It comes in whole or ground form.

- ❋ Cumin is used as a stomach tonic, antioxidant, and is being studied as a possible cancer fighting agent. Cumin tea helps with gastrointestinal problems. A cumin plaster will eliminate growths and reduce swelling.

curry

Curry, native to India and the Far East, is a blend of several spices including ginger, chili, coriander, cinnamon, fenugreek, turmeric, mustard, pepper, and cloves. The blends vary depending on the dish. Curry is used in breads, soups, salad dressings, sauces, dips, marinades, casseroles, beef, lamb, poultry, fish, seafood, fruit, vegetables, and rice.

- ❋ Curry, because it is a mixture of many herbs, is not used as a medicinal herb.

fenugreek
(*Trigonella foenumgraecum*)

Fenugreek, indigenous to Asia, is an annual member of the pea family with seeds that have a slightly bitter, caramel flavor.
It is used in imitation maple flavoring, curry powder, and chutney. Fenugreek is available in whole and ground seeds.

- ❋ Fenugreek is used as an expectorant and stomach tonic. Fenugreek tea is good for bronchitis, fevers, and for a sore throat. The seed aids the gastrointestinal system. A poultice may be applied to cuts, sores, and skin irritations.

ginger
(*Zingiber officinale*)

Ginger, indigenous to the Asian tropics, is a perennial root with a hot, sweet flavor. Whole ginger is used in beverages, tea, ginger beer, syrups, marinades, preserves, stewed fruit, pickling, and teriyaki sauce. Ground ginger is used in appetizers, breads, soups, salads, salad dressings, sauces, beef, poultry, lamb, pork, fruits, vegetables, sweet potatoes, fruit pies, and ice cream. Available fresh in whole root or in dried ground form.

- Ginger is used as an appetizer, stimulant, and as an aid to the immune system. A daily sprinkle of ginger, best taken in coffee, tea, or other hot drink, will boost the immune system and help prevent colds and flu. Hot ginger tea will also sooth a sore throat, promote sweating to break a fever, helps with gastrointestinal problems, and encourages menstruation. A pinch of ginger or a small piece of ginger root will stimulate the salivary glands and relieve dry mouth.
- To make bruised ginger, break the skin without breaking the root by pounding gently with a meat tenderizer.

mace
(Myristica fragrans)

Mace, native to the Maluku (Moluccas) Island of Indonesia, is the grainy membrane that covers the shell of the nutmeg seed and has a flavor similar to nutmeg.
Mace is used in breads, doughnuts, pancakes, waffles, muffins, coffee cakes, pound cake, spice cake, devil's food cake, gingerbread, Danish pastries, frostings, glazes, fruit salads, fruit salad dressing, fruit pies, cream cheese, white sauces, poultry, beef, lamb, fish, apple and cherry dishes. Mace is available whole and in ground form.

- Mace has medicinal properties similar to those of nutmeg. See nutmeg.

mustard
(Brassica hirta)

Mustard, native to Europe, is a member of the mustard family with yellow flowers and pods, and small round seeds.
Mustard seed is used in pickles, salad dressings, corned beef, boiled cabbage and sauerkraut. Dry mustard is used to make mustard sauce, in appetizers, salad dressings, sauces, egg and cheese dishes, poultry, meats, and vegetables. Mustard comes in three varieties, yellow or white *(Brassica hirta),* brown *(Brassica juncea),* and black *(Brassica nigra).* Mustard is available as mustard seed and dry mustard.

- Mustard is used as a diuretic, laxative, and stimulant. A cup of mustard tea, taken quickly, will induce vomiting. Small servings of tea will increase appetite and help with intestinal problems. A plaster, made with flour and egg whites, may be applied to the kidney area for irritated kidneys.
- Do not leave the plaster on for very long and never apply to sensitive skin.

nutmeg
(Myristica fragrans)

Nutmeg, indigenous to the Maluku, is the core of the seed of the evergreen tropical nutmeg tree. Nutmeg is used in breads, cakes, cookies, fruit salads, fruit salad dressing, fruit pies, poultry, beef, lamb, fish, apple and cherry dishes. It is also used in making cola soft drinks and egg nog. It is available in whole and ground form.

- Nutmeg is used as an expectorant and stomach tonic. In small amounts, nutmeg relieves indigestion and prevents gas. It also encourages menstrual flow.
- Nutmeg is a mild hallucinogen. When using nutmeg medicinally, use only in small amounts. Eating only two nutmegs can be fatal! Keep out of children's reach. Some symptoms of poisoning are abdominal pain, blurred or double vision, and incoherence.

pepper
(Piper nigrum)

Pepper corns, native to the East Indies, are the dried berries of the pepper vine and have a hot bite to them.

Pepper corns are used in just about every dish in every culture. Pepper comes in four varieties, green, black, red, and white (the inside portion of the black peppercorn).

Pepper is available in whole peppercorns and in ground form.

- ❀ Pepper is used as a stimulant and, in small amounts, it is good for gastrointestinal problems. To remove blockage from one nostril, place a small pinch just inside the other nostril to promote sneezing. This should effectively clear the blocked nostril and works especially well in toddlers who have a tendency to stuff things up their noses!

❀ Health benefits of specific herb.
✎ Note or explanation.

Always steep herb teas.
Never boil.
Never use aluminum pots or pans to prepare tea.

Wine Connoisseur

Cooking with wine is an age-old tradition and with good reason. Wine complements the flavor and aroma of food and enhances the distinguishing characteristics of almost any dish. Just a splash of wine lends a rich, distinctive flavor to entrees, marinades, soups, and stews. In fact, wine will not only bring out the flavor in meat, it is a great tenderizer. Wine also adds a subtle, enticing quality to sweet breads, cakes, cookies, and other desserts.

Wines are made from freshly squeezed grape juice. No additives or preservatives are necessary because the juice is naturally preserved through fermentation. During this process of aging, wine develops its own personality, which is a combination of smoothness, mellowness, aroma, and flavor.

The aging period is determined by the variety of the wine and is not necessarily indicative of the quality of the wine. Some wines reach maturity in a few months while others take years to develop their optimum bouquet and flavor, but the majority of wines fall somewhere in between.

Good quality table wines are widely available and priced to suit just about any budget. But, before you shop, keep in mind that an expensive wine is not necessarily better. A good wine usually runs somewhere between $7.00 and $30.00 for a 750 ml bottle.

There are five primary categories of wine: appetizer, dessert, red, sparkling wines, and white wines. They are also classified according to similar characteristics: appetizer, dessert, generic, sparkling, and varietal. In addition, wines are grouped by the amount of natural sugar in them or how sweet they taste and rank from very dry to sweet. The following guide gives a basic idea of what the terms mean:

- ❖ A *very dry/brut* champagne has a trace of natural sugar. These champagnes lack sweetness and are described in terms of crispness.

- ❖ A *dry/sec* wine or champagne contains a very small amount of natural sugar but does not taste sweet to most people. These champagnes are described in terms of sharpness.

- ❖ A *medium dry/demi-sec* wine or champagne has a fair amount of natural sugar and a lightly sweet flavor.

- ❖ A *medium sweet/doux* wine or champagne contains a good amount of natural sugar and is sweet to the taste.

- ❖ A *sweet/moelleux* wine has the highest content of natural sugar and tastes very sweet.

Dishes and Complementary Wines

Customarily, the same wine that is used to prepare a dish should be served with it so that there is no conflict in flavor and aroma. A less expensive wine may be used in making the dish but always select a good quality table wine for serving.

Appetizer/soup Dry or medium-dry wines:
Madeira, red wine, sherry, and white wine.

Dessert/fruits Medium sweet or sweet wines:
Muscat, Port, sauterne, sherry, Champagne, and sparkling Burgundy.

Egg or cheese	<u>Dry or medium dry wines:</u> Burgundy, Bordeaux, Merlot, and pinot noir.
Fish	<u>Dark meat:</u> Claret, rosé, and vin rosé. <u>White meat or shellfish:</u> Dry and medium-dry white wines.
Game	<u>Dry or medium dry red wines:</u> Burgundy and sherry.
Meat	<u>Dry or medium dry red wines:</u> Bordeaux, Burgundy, Cabernet sauvignon, Merlot, Muscatel, rosé, and zinfandel.
Poultry	<u>Dry or medium dry white wines:</u> Sherry, Muscatel, and rosé.
Sauces	<u>Brown:</u> Dry wines. Riesling, sherry, and white wine. <u>Cheese or tomato:</u> Dry wines. Riesling, sherry, and white wine. <u>Dessert or sweet:</u> Sweet wines. Muscatel, port, sherry, and white wine. <u>White:</u> Dry white wines. Riesling, and sherry.

✎ Cooking sherries and wines contain salt, so your recipe may need to be adjusted accordingly. By using a good table wine, you can avoid this problem and have a wider variety to choose from. Store wines laying down in a cool place that is out of direct sunlight.

Dinner Wines

appetizer	<u>Dry or medium dry wines:</u> Madeira, red wine, sherry, and white wine.
dessert	<u>Sweet or medium sweet wines:</u> Madeira, Muscat, port, Champagne, sauterne, and sparkling Burgundy. (Serve a wine that is sweeter than the dessert, or the wine will taste bitter.)
generic	<u>Dry red wines:</u> Burgundy, Chianti, and claret. <u>Medium dry red wines:</u> Rosé and vin rosé.

<u>Medium sweet red wines:</u>
Barbera, vino rosso, and rosé.

<u>Dry white wines:</u>
Chablis and Sauterne.

<u>Medium dry white wines:</u>
Chianti, Haut Sauterne.

<u>Sweet white wines:</u>
Sauterne.

sparkling <u>Champagnes:</u>

<u>Medium dry to sweet:</u>
Pink Champagne.

<u>Sweet:</u>
Cold duck and sparkling Burgundy.

<u>Sweet Muscat:</u>
Asti Spumante, moscato Ababile, moscato Spumante, and sparkling Muscat.

varietal <u>Dry red wines:</u>
Cabernet, ruby cabernet, cabernet sauvignon, Merlot, pinot noir, and zinfandel.

<u>Sweet red wines:</u>
Cabernet sauvignon, sherry, zinfandel.

<u>Dry to medium sweet rosés:</u>
Cabernet rosé, Grenache rosé, and zinfandel rosé.

<u>Dry white wines:</u>
Chardonnay, chenin blanc, pinot blanc, Riesling, dry Semillon, sauvignon blanc, and voignier.

<u>Sweet white wines:</u>
Muscat bordelaise and sweet Semillon.

Wines and Serving Temperatures

Choose your wines well before an event and cool them accordingly, so that they will be ready to serve. A medium dry wine is best for a large number of guests because it should suit everyone.

red room temperature
pink cool
white chill (white wines tend to lose their bouquet when too cold)
champagne & chill at 45 degrees F (7.2 degrees C)
   sparkling wines

Reading a Wine Label

Whether domestic or imported, wine labels bear the same general information: the name of the grape from which the wine was made, the region where it was grown, the name of the vineyard, and the year it was bottled. In addition to this, the labels on vintage and high quality wines include a more precise description of the wine.

The quality of a fine Bordeaux is based on the Médoc Classification of 1855. According to this system, a Bordeaux is classified as 1 er cru or 1 er grand cru, meaning that the grapes were taken from the first and thereby the best harvest. The ranking continues from there, with the 5 em cru being the fifth growth and therefore the fifth in quality. Of course, there are many wine critics who disagree with the Médoc classification system and believe that it should be updated. Still, it is the standard of ranking a Bordeaux.

The information in this segment will help you to interpret a vintage wine label and apply that knowledge to your cooking and entertaining skills. With some practice and wine-tasting experience, you will become familiar with wines, more confident in your choices, and be well on your way to being able to distinguish between a passable wine and an excellent one.

The vintage wine labels I have chosen as examples were taken from the actual bottles. I found this information and examples in some of my father's notes, many years ago.

Our first example is the label on a bottle of vintage Bordeaux which reads:

Château Haut-Brion
Premier Grand Cru Classe
Appelation Graves Controlee
1949
Mise en Bouteilles ou Château

Based on this information, we know that this particular wine is a product of the Château Haut-Brion vineyards in the district of Graves, France. It is a Grand Cru which means that it is from the best growth and is therefore an excellent wine.

The Bordeaux was bottled in 1949 and, according to the last line on the label, it was bottled at the Chateau itself.

Our second example is displayed on a bottle of vintage Hock:

1952
Rheingau
Rauenthaler Burggarten
Riesling Spatlese
Originalabfullung Weingut Diefenhardt

    This Hock was bottled in 1952. It came from the Burggarten vineyards at Rauenthal in the Rhinegau region of Germany. The Riesling grapes were gathered after the main and best harvest, and bottled at the Diefenhardt vineyard.

    Upon further examination of the bottle, we find that the name of the vineyard, the owner's name, and the year the wine was bottled have been burned into the cork. This imprint is known as a Korkbrand. Only the very finest German wines have these Korkbrands, which are a guarantee of quality.

    These wines are two of the rarest and most superb wines in the world. The quality of the grapes and their careful handling guaranteed that the wine would age well. Exceptionally fine wines, such as these, run into the thousands of dollars!

= Equivalents & Substitutions =

Oven and Cooking Temperatures

Heat	Temperature	
	(F)	(C)
broil	550	290
very hot	450	230
hot	400	205
moderately hot	375	190
moderate	350	175
moderately low	325	165
low	300	150
very low	200	95

Temperature Conversions

These are the freezing and boiling points of water at sea level:

Freezing: 0 degrees C = 32 degrees F

Boiling: 100 degrees C = 212 degrees F

Use the following equations to convert from one scale to the other

    degrees F = 9/5 degrees C + 32 degrees

    degrees C = 5/9 (degrees F – 32 degrees C)

(Remember to do the work within the parenthesis first.)

Dry and Liquid Measure Equivalents

This list gives the amount of a dry ingredient and its corresponding volume equivalent, which comes in handy when following certain recipes.

Dry Measure	Volume Equivalent	International System (SI)
3 tsp.	1 Tbsp.	45 g
4 Tbsp.	1/4 c.	50 g
5 1/3 Tbsp.	1/3 c.	75 g
1 sq. baking chocolate	1 oz.	25 g
5 c. grated cheese	1 lb.	450 g
3 c. cornmeal	1 lb.	450 g
4 c. flour	1 lb.	450 g
2 1/3 c. enriched rice	1 lb.	450 g

Liquid Measure	Volume Equivalent	International System (IS)
2 Tbsp.	1 fl. oz.	25 ml
6 Tbsp.	1 c. (8 fl. oz.)	225 ml
2 c.	1 pint (16 oz. or 1 lb.)	450 ml
2 pints	1 quart (32 oz.)	1 liter
4 quarts	1 gallon (128 oz.)	3 3/4 liters

Substitutions

The following ingredients can be substituted for use in cooking or baking:

Ingredient	Substitution
1 c. ricotta cheese	1 c. cottage cheese
1 sq. baking chocolate (1 oz.)	3 Tbsp. cocoa powder and 1Tbsp. shortening, butter, or margarine
1 c. crushed, dry bread crumbs	1 c. crushed corn flakes or crackers
1 Tbsp. cornstarch	1 Tbsp. enriched flour
1 garlic clove	1/8 tsp. garlic powder
1 c. sour cream	1 c. plain yogurt and 1/2 tsp. cornstarch
1 Tbsp. fresh herbs	1 tsp. dry herbs
1/2 c. fresh herbs	1 Tbsp. dry herbs
1 lemon or lime rind	1 1/2 Tbsp. dry zest
1 c. sour milk	1 c. milk and 1 Tbsp. Lemon juice or vinegar
1 Tbsp. prepared mustard	1 tsp. dry mustard and 1/2 tsp. vinegar
1/2 c. chopped nuts	1/2 c. old fashioned oatmeal
1 small onion	1 Tbsp. dry onion flakes
1 c. tomato juice	1/2 c. catsup and 1/2 c. water
1 cake compressed yeast	1 pkg. active dry yeast
1 pkg. active dry yeast	2 tsp. active dry yeast

Dry to Cooked Measurements

The following is a list of dry food measurements and the quantity of cooked food that can be made from these amounts:

Dry Measure	Cooked Foods
1 c. beans	6 c. beans
2 c. macaroni	4 c. macaroni
1 lb. pasta	8 c. pasta
2 1/2 c. instant potatoes	4 c. mashed potatoes
1 1/2 c. enriched rice	4 c. rice
2 c. instant rice	4 c. rice

 Meal Planner

The following chart is a buying guide and is based on four servings:

Food	Amount Needed (based on 4 servings)
dairy	
cottage cheese	1 pint
ice cream, sherbet	1 pint
milk	1 quart
natural or process cheese	8 ounces
sour cream or yogurt	1 pint
fish	
seafood (in shell)	4 lbs.
seafood or fish fillets	2 lbs.
fruits	
canned or frozen	1 lb.
dehydrated	1 cup
fresh: apples, apricots, bananas, berries, grapes, peaches, pears, or plums	1 lb.
fresh citrus: grapefruit, oranges, etc.	2 lb.
grains	
cornmeal	1 cup
hot wheat cereals	3/4 cups
hominy grits, oatmeal	1 1/2 cups
enriched rice	1 1/2 cups
instant rice	2 cups
meats	
beef, game, lamb or pork cuts	2 lbs.
ground meat	1 lb.
pasta	
egg noodles	2 cups
macaroni	2 cups
penne	2 cups
spaghetti	8 ounces

Food	Amount Needed (based on 4 servings)
poultry	
whole: chicken, Cornish game hens, game birds, or duck	3 lbs.
pieces: chicken, duck or turkey	3 lbs.
boneless: chicken, duck, or turkey breasts	2 lbs.
vegetables	
canned or frozen	1 lb.
instant potatoes	2 1/2 cups
legumes: beans, lentils,	2 cups
or split peas	1 lb.
fresh: green beans, beets, broccoli, cabbage, carrots, cauliflower, corn on the cob, lettuce, potatoes, or turnips	1 lb.
fresh: peas or snow peas, spinach, squash, or tomatoes	2 lbs.

Food Storage & Safety

Because bacteria grows quickly at room temperature, precautions need to be taken to avoid accidental poisoning. This section contains information that will help you handle food safely.

Shop Safely

- ✓ If you plan to run other errands after shopping, take a cooler along for items that need to be kept cold or frozen.

- ✓ Check packages for cuts or tears.

- ✓ Check cans to make sure they are not dented or swollen.

- ✓ Check the lids on jars. They should be tightly sealed. The center of the lid will be depressed. If the lid pops up after you push it down, it is not sealed.

- ✓ Make sure that frozen foods are solid.

- ✓ If foods are labeled "keep refrigerated", they should be in the refrigerated section or kept cold.

- ✓ Buy foods before their expiration date.

- ✓ Buy meats last. Place them in plastic bags to prevent blood from dripping on other foods.

Food Handling Basics

- ✓ Freeze meats and fish immediately. Place in airtight plastic freezer bags or wrap securely in aluminum foil or freezer wrap.

- ✓ Place refrigerated items so that air circulates freely around them.

- ✓ Wrap meat tightly and place in refrigerated meat bin or the bottom of the refrigerator so that it stays cold and blood does not drip on other foods.

- ✓ Follow safe handling information on packaging.

- ✓ Throw out any foods that have been in the refrigerator for a while or that smell strange.

- ✓ Never taste any food to see if it is still good. "When in doubt, throw it out."

- ✓ Store canned and bottled foods in a cool, dark place.

Refrigerator and Freezer Shelf Life

Fresh and frozen foods should be kept in the refrigerator or freezer in airtight wrapping or containers. The refrigerator should be set at 40 degrees F (5 degrees C) and the freezer at 0 degrees F (-18 degrees C).

Approximate refrigerator shelf life, in days, weeks, and/or months, is followed by that for the freezer (❄).

Food	Days	Weeks	Months
bacon		1	❄ 1
breast milk	5		❄ 4
butter		2	❄ 6
buttermilk		2	do not freeze
canned ham (unopened)		9	do not freeze
cheese			
hard		4	❄ 6
cottage cheese		1	❄ 3
cream cheese		2	❄ 2
process cheese		1	❄ 6
corned beef			
(in pickling juices)		1	❄ 1
cream		2	❄ 2
eggs			
fresh		2	do not freeze
hard boiled		1	do not freeze
raw yolks or whites	4		❄ 1
liquid pasteurized		2	❄ 1
or egg substitute			
fish			
fillet or	2		❄ 6
seafood			
frozen entrees	0		❄ 4
fruit			
fresh: apples		1	
berries		2	
citrus		1	
frozen			
all			❄ 8
ham			
whole, fully cooked		1	❄ 2
half, fully cooked	5		❄ 2
hard sausage			
Italian, pepperoni,		3	❄ 2
Polish or salami			
hot dogs/sandwich meats		2	❄ 4
(sealed package)			

Food	Days	Weeks	Months
ice cream			❄ 3
infant formula (prepared)	2		do not freeze
meat beef cuts	3		❄ 9
lamb cuts	3		❄ 9
pork or veal cuts	3		❄ 6
ground meats	2		❄ 6
poultry			
whole chicken or turkey	2		❄ 9
sectioned chicken or turkey	2		❄ 9
reconstituted milk condensed, dry, or evaporated	5		do not freeze
sausage			
raw beef, pork or turkey	2		❄ 2
smoked links or or patties		1	❄ 2
sour cream		2	do not freeze
yogurt		1	do not freeze

Pantry Shelf Life

These foods will keep on the shelf if the storage area is kept cool (72 degrees F, 22 degrees C), dark, and dry.

avocados	1 week	**cereals/crackers**	4 months
bananas/tomatoes	5 days	**dehydrated fruits/vegetables**	1 year
garlic/onions/potatoes	2 months	**pasta/rice**	1 year
bread	4 days	**canned foods**	1 year

Thawing and Marinating

✓ Do not thaw meat, fish, or poultry on the counter. Place well wrapped fish or poultry in cold water, check the water often, and keep it cold. May also be defrosted in microwave.

✓ Shellfish and seafood should be thawed in cold water just before use. Strain and pat dry.

✓ Meat and poultry may be thawed overnight in the refrigerator or in the microwave on the defrost setting. Poultry needs to be thoroughly thawed before cooking.

✓ Never marinate at room temperature. Place food to be marinated in the refrigerator overnight or store in an airtight container in the freezer for later use.

✓ Throw out any leftover marinade or bring to a boil and use as a sauce on cooked meat.

Preparing to Cook

✓ Remove jewelry, such as rings and watches, and wash your hands well before handling food. Wash your hands again between working with meats, and fruits or vegetables. If you leave the kitchen or handle anything that is not clean, wash your hands again.

✓ Wash all utensils and surfaces with hot soapy water after working with raw meat and do not let the juices come into contact with other foods.

✓ It is best to use separate cutting boards for meats and fruits or vegetables.

✓ Use a scrub brush to eliminate wax and pesticides from fruits and vegetables. Do this under cold running water. Delicate fruits and vegetables can be cleaned by rubbing or using a soft scrub brush.

✓ When barbecuing, do not use the same platter for cooked meats and raw meats.

Tips

✓ Scrape out avocados, tomatoes, and kiwi with a grapefruit spoon or thin bowled teaspoon. For avocado slices, quarter the avocado lengthwise, peel it, then slice it.

✓ To keep avocado dishes such as guacamole from discoloring, place an avocado bone in the bottom of the serving bowl.

✓ Bring water to a boil before adding eggs for easy to peel hard boiled eggs and boil 20 minutes.

✓ Hard boiled eggs will keep in the refrigerator for three to four days.

✓ Place peeled onions in ice water before slicing or dicing and breath through your mouth, to avoid eye and nose irritation.

- ✓ To keep pudding or custard from forming a crust, place plastic wrap or wax paper on surface.

- ✓ Ripen green tomatoes at room temperature in a paper sack or in a cool, dark cabinet.

- ✓ Place a few bay leaves in the bottom of flour and grain bins to repel weevils.

- ✓ Charcoal briquettes work as well as baking soda to eliminate refrigerator odor.

- ✓ To remove chili juice from hands after peeling chili or working with it, rinse hands in lemon juice or vinegar then wash with cool, soapy water.

- ✓ Prepare two or three times the amount of food needed for a meal and freeze extras in airtight containers for a later date. Heat them up for quick and easy meals on those extra busy days.

Keeping it Clean

- ✓ Wash cutting boards with a solution of one part bleach and nine parts water.

- ✓ Soak sponges in bleach solution every two weeks and replace them every four months.

- ✓ It is best to use dishcloths instead of sponges because you can use them then toss them in the laundry. Change out dishcloths and kitchen towels at least once daily.

- ✓ Keep your refrigerator and microwave oven clean by wiping them out regularly with hot soap water. It's a lot easier than having to scrub off built-up food and grime right before your company arrives.

Safe Cooking Temperatures

Eggs, meat, poultry, and fish need to be cooked before eating. Cooking food thoroughly keeps bacteria from growing. It is also advisable to drink only pasteurized milk.

To check the temperature of meat, pierce through the thickest part with a meat thermometer. Do not touch the sides or bottom of the pan, the bone, or the fat.

Meat Product	Internal/Cooked Temperature	
	(F)	(C)
beef, veal, lamb		
ground	160	70
roasts/steaks		
well-done	170	80
medium	160	70
medium rare	145	65

* Cook ground meats until no longer pink.

ham		
fully cooked	140	60
raw shank	160	70
pork		
ground and cuts		
well-done	170	80
medium	160	70
poultry		
ground	165	75
whole, unstuffed		
well-done	180	85
medium	170	80
whole, stuffed	180	85
pieces	170	80

* Cook until juices run clear.

Serving Safety

✓ Use clean platters and utensils for serving.

✓ Do not keep cooked foods at room temperature for longer than two hours.

✓ Keep hot foods hot through the use of a slow cooker or fondue dish.

✓ Keep cold foods cold by keeping them on ice.

✓ When refreshing serving trays, keep fresh foods separated from foods that have been setting out for a while.

Leftovers

✓ Throw out any food that seems questionable. "When in doubt, throw it out."

✓ Refrigerate or freeze foods within two hours after cooking.

✓ If a food keeps well in the freezer, seal it well and freeze it for another time.

✓ To reheat, make sure that the food is heated evenly and steaming hot.

🔪 Some bacteria are beneficial to us, such as that in yogurt, buttermilk, and cheese. Harmful bacteria, on the other hand, needs to be eliminated through proper food handling.
Food poisoning symptoms (vomiting, diarrhea, fever, or cramps) show up within 4 to 48 hours after eating contaminated food. If you suspect that you may have food poisoning, get medical help immediately.

Grocery List

The following grocery list is not intended for the kitchen alone, but covers household and pet items as well. It comes in handy when writing out your grocery list and as a guideline for stocking up.

This comprehensive list has some items that many people do not use, but they have been included for those who do. There is also plenty of space to customize it to your own lifestyle.

Baking Ingredients

Baking chocolate:
bitter-sweet squares	milk chocolate squares/chips
chocolate covered espresso beans	semi-sweet squares/chips/mini's
cocoa powder	unsweetened squares
German's sweet squares	white chocolate squares/chips

Cake mixes:
angel food	devil's food	yellow	frosting
carrot	specialty	white	decors/sprinkles/candles

Dried fruit:
apples	coconut	peaches	raisins/golden raisins
apricots	cranberries	prunes	coated raisins

Flour:
all-purpose	cornmeal	rye flour	wheat germ
buckwheat	oatmeal	self-rising	whole wheat
cake flour	rice flour	semolina	

Gelatin:
flavored	lite	plain

Leavening agents:
baking powder	baking soda	yeast

Nuts:
almonds	macadamia	pecans	pistachios
cashews	peanuts	piñons (pine nuts)	walnuts

Oils & Shortening:
canola	corn	peanut	sesame
cooking spray	olive	safflower	vegetable
shortening	butter-flavored shortening		unsalted butter

The Ultimate Kitchen Consultant

Puddings:

banana	chocolate	custard	vanilla
butterscotch	coconut	lemon	

Salt:

iodized	kosher	rock	sea

Seasonings:

allspice	coconut extract	whole nutmeg	spearmint extract
almond extract	coriander	dried onions	summer savory
anchovy paste	cream of tarter	orange extract	tarragon
anise seed	cumin	orange zest	thyme
basil	curry powder	oregano	vanilla beans
bay leaves	dill	paprika	vanilla extract
ground black pepper	fennel	parsley	light vanilla extract
bouillon	garlic powder	pepper corns	vegetable seasoning
cayenne	ginger	poppy seed	
chili powder	lemon extract	rosemary	
chives	lemon zest	saffron	
ground cinnamon	lime zest	sage	
cinnamon sticks	marjoram	seasoned salt	
ground cloves	meat tenderizer	sesame seed	
whole cloves	ground nutmeg	spearmint	

Sugar:

brown	granulated	raw
cubes	powdered	sugar substitute

Thickeners:

arrowroot	corn starch	fruit pectin

Vinegars:

apple cider	distilled	raspberry	red wine
balsamic	herb	rice	white wine

Beverages

Coffee:

coffee beans	de-caf	espresso	ground coffee
instant	specialty coffees		

Cold drinks:

club soda	cola	fruit flavored	lemon-lime
miscellaneous	seltzer		

Cold drink mixes:

instant breakfast	fruit drink powder	nutritional supplement

Drink additives:

non-dairy creamer	half-and-half	honey	lemon juice/wedges
marshmallows	sugar (cubes/granulated)	sugar substitute	whipped cream

Juices:

apple	grape	limeade	prune
apple cider	grapefruit	key lime (reconstituted)	
apricot nectar	juice blends	mango	tomato
cherry cider	lemon (reconstituted)	orange	vegetable
clam juice	lemonade	papaya	
cranberry	lime (reconstituted)	pineapple	

Hot drink mixes:

hot cider	hot cocoa	orange drink powder

Liquor:

beer	cognac	rum	whiskey
brandy	gin	schnapps	wine
fruit brandy	liqueurs	vodka	

Mixes & garnishes:

celery	lemons	Margarita mix	triple sec
daiquiri mix	limes	spearmint sprigs	
grenadine syrup	sweetened lime juice	sweet and sour mix	specialty mixers
kiwis	Maraschino cherries	tonic water	and liqueurs

Tea:

decaffeinated	green tea	instant	specialty
flavored teas	herbal	regular	

Water:

bottled water	Perrier	seltzer	sparkling

Breads

Breads:

bread crumbs	donuts	phyllo dough	wraps
canned biscuits	French bread	sandwich bread	
croutons	muffins	stuffing	
dinner rolls	pie crusts	tortillas (flour/corn)	

Chips:

cheese puffs	corn chips	potato chips	pretzels

Cookies:

butter	dark chocolate wafers	macaroons	sandwich
chocolate chip	ginger snaps	oatmeal	vanilla wafers

Crackers:

animal	cheese	party assortment	whole grain
arrowroot	graham	rye	

Cereal

Hot:

baby cereal	bran	flavored	oatmeal
barley	farina	instant	whole wheat

Cold:

bran	granola	pre-sweetened	whole wheat
corn flakes	oat	puffed rice	
flavored	natural	puffed oats	

Dairy

Cheese:

American	Colby	Gruyere	process cheese
St. Andre	cottage cheese	Limburger	ricotta
blue cheese	cream cheese	longhorn	Romano
brick cheese	Edam	montrachet	Roquefort
Brie	Emmenthal	mozzarella	Swiss
Camembert	feta	Muenster	
cheddar	gjetost	mysost	sandwich slices
chevre	Gouda	Parmesan	

Dips:

French onion	green onion	jalapeño	salsa
green chili	guacamole	pico de gallo	spinach

Ice cream:

assorted flavors	sherbet	assorted treats	frozen yogurt

Milk:

butter milk	dry milk	half-and-half	soy milk
cream	evaporated milk	infant formula	whipping cream

Yogurt:

Plain	flavored

Fish & Seafood

Canned:

anchovies	crab	sardines	tuna
caviar	salmon	shrimp	

Fresh:

bass	frog legs	octopus	sole
calamari	grouper	oysters	squid
caviar	haddock	perch	swordfish
clams	herring	salmon	talapia
cod	lobster tails	scallops	trout
crab	mackerel	shad	
cuttle fish	mahimahi	shrimp	
eel	mussels	smelts	

Fruit

Canned fruits:

apricots	cherries	peaches	plums
blackberries	fruit cocktail	pears	raspberries
blueberries	gooseberries	pie filling	strawberries
boysenberries	mandarin oranges	pineapple	baby food

Fresh fruit:

apples	currants	nectarines	star fruit (carambola)
apricots	elderberries	oranges	strawberries
bananas	grapefruit	papaya	tangelos
blackberries	grapes	passion fruit	tangerines
blueberries	guava	peaches	watermelon
boysenberries	honey dew	pears	
cantaloupe	kiwi	pineapple	
casaba	kumquats	plums	
cherries	lemons	pomegranates	
coconut	limes	quince	
cranberries	mangos	raspberries	

Frozen fruits:

berry mixture	blueberries	melon chunks	raspberries
blackberries	boysenberries	peaches	strawberries

Meats

Canned meats:
chopped ham	ham	potted meat	Vienna sausages
corned beef	pate de foie	tongue	baby food

Fresh & Frozen meats:

Beef
brains	hamburger patties	roast	stew meat
brisket	heart	short ribs	tongue
ground beef	liver	steak	tripe

Mutton
leg	loin	roast	stew meat

Ostrich

Pork
bacon	ground pork	leg
chops	ham	roast

Rabbit

Sausages
chorizo	Polish	turkey sausage
Italian	pork sausage	wieners

Veal

Pasta, Rice, & Beans

Pasta:
fettuccini	manicotti	rigatoni	hamburger/tuna meals
garden rotini	mostaccioli	rotelle	macaroni & cheese
jumbo shells	noodles	rotini	pasta dinners
lasagna	penne	spaghetti	
macaroni	ramen noodles	vermicelli	

Rice:
brown	converted	long grain	wild

Beans/legumes:
black-eyed peas	kidney beans	lentils	small white beans
chick peas (garbanzos)	lima beans	pinto beans	split peas

Poultry

Chicken:
breasts	gizzards	thighs	whole
drumsticks	livers	wings	

Duck

Eggs:
fresh farm	quail	egg substitute	
duck	white	powdered eggs	

Game:
dove	game hens	pheasant	quail

Turkey:
breast	legs	smoked	whole

Sauces & Dressings

Dressings:
blue cheese	Italian	Russian	
French	ranch	thousand island	

Sauces:
barbecue	oyster	salsa	Tabasco
Béchamel	picante	soy	Worcestershire
brisket	pico de gallo	steak	

Soups

beef bouillon	cheese	chowders	potato
beef consume	chicken bouillon	cream soups	tomato
beef stew	chicken consume	minestrone	vegetable

Snacks & Gum

candy bars	energy bars	mixed nuts	gum
candy mix	fruit rolls/bars	popcorn	sugarless gum
dinner mints	granola bars		

Spreads, Syrups, & Condiments

Spreads:
butter	jelly	mayonnaise	preserves
jam	margarine	peanut butter	sandwich spread

Syrups:
blackberry	caramel	maple	strawberry
blueberry	chocolate	molasses	
boysenberry	honey	raspberry	

Condiments:
chutney	Dijon mustard	pickle relish
catsup	yellow mustard	

Vegetables & Other Produce

Canned:
artichoke hearts	corn	jalapeños	small white potatoes
asparagus	creamed corn	kidney beans	Spanish olives
baked beans	dill pickles	kosher dills	tomato paste
beets	French green beans	mushrooms	tomato sauce
black olives	gherkins	marinated mushrooms	
bread & butter pickles	green beans	peas	whole tomatoes
capers	green chili	pearl onions	yellow hots
carrots	hot mix	pumpkin	

Dried:
mushrooms	potatoes	tomatoes

Fresh:
artichoke	celery	lettuce	shallots
asparagus	chili	mushrooms	snow peas
beets	cilantro	okra	spearmint
avocados	corn on the cob	onions	spinach
bell peppers	cucumbers	pablano peppers	squash
broccoli	escarole	parsley	sweet potatoes
Brussels sprouts	ginger root	potatoes	tomatoes
cabbage	jalapeños	radicchio	watercress
carrots	kelp (sea weed)	salad mix	zucchini
cauliflower	leeks	scallions	

Frozen:
breaded vegetables	California mix	corn	hash browns
broccoli	carrots	corn on the cob	okra
Brussels sprouts	cauliflower	French fries	peas/snow peas
baby corn	chili	green beans	spinach

Health & Beauty

Antiseptics:
alcohol	gentian violet	miscellaneous
anti-biotic ointment	iodine	peroxide

Baby items:
bottles	diaper rash ointment	lotion	training pants/pull-ups
disposable bottles	diapers/reg. or disposable	nursing pads	wipes
disposable bottle liners	oil	powder	

Bandages:
adhesive tape (various widths)	bandage strips	4X4 gauze pads	safety pins
ace bandages (various sizes)	2X2 gauze pads	liquid bandage	

Bath:
bath oil	hand soap	lotion	bath towels
body wash	liquid hand soap	cream	hand towels
bubble bath	sun screen	wash cloths	

Hair:
accessories	conditioning treatment	gel/hair spray	permanent
brush/comb	creme rinse	hair color	

Medications:
allergy/sinus	children/infant's cold medicine	laxatives
antacids	children/infant's fever reducer	motion sickness tabs
anti-diarrheal	cough drops/syrup	pain reliever
baby teething gel	flu medicine	prescription medications

Miscellaneous:
floss	disposable razors	feminine napkins	eye drops
mouthwash	hair removal cream/wax	panty liners	lens cleaner
tooth brushes	shaver/head replacements	tampons	saline solution
toothpaste	shaving cream		

Nails:
cotton balls	file/buffer	polish remover	nail clippers
polish	scissors		

Vitamins & Supplements:
Children's vitamins	infant vitamins	supplements	herbal supplements
multiple vitamins			

Household Goods

Cleansers:

abrasive cleanser	dish soap	rust and lime remover
air freshener	dishwasher detergent	RV tank treatment
carpet cleaner/freshener	fabric softener	stain remover
bleach	laundry detergent	

Kitchen supplies:

bottle brush	kitchen scissors	pot holders/mitts	vacuum cleaner bags
broom	kitchen towels	scrub pads	vegetable brush
dish cloths	mop	trash bags	

Office:

cassette tapes	computer paper	envelopes	postage stamps
CD's	diskettes	memory cards	8mm tapes
computer ink	DVD's	photo film	VHS tapes

Paper goods:

aluminum foil	paper plates	plastic wrap	bath tissue
coffee filters	paper napkins	sandwich bags	marine bath tissue
freezer bags/paper	paper towels	storage boxes	
paper cups/glasses	parchment paper	wax paper	

Sewing:

needles	scissors	thread
safety pins	straight pins	

Utility:

batteries	lamp oil/wicks	duck tape	scotch tape
flashlight/ bulbs	lighters	masking tape	
light bulbs	matches	packaging tape	

Pet supplies

House pets:

bedding	cat litter	hamster food	water conditioner
collar	fish flakes	turtle food	
cat/dog food	flea collar/drops	vitamin drops	

Equestrian:

bran	hay	salt block	vitamins
corn	oats	sweet feed	
antibiotics	first-aid supplies	needles	syringes
hoof clippers	hoof pick	hoof protectant	hoof rasp
brush	curry comb	shampoo	bedding
coat luster	mane & tail comb		
belly strap	hackamore	lead rope	saddle
bridle	halter	lunge rope	saddle bags
cinch	lariat	lunge whip	saddle blanket

Yard & Garden

bulbs	garden hose	peat moss/potting soil	pond supplies
bulb planter	gardening tools	planters	seeds
fertilizer	insecticide	plant food/root stimulator	starters
garden gloves	irrigation supplies	pool supplies	weed killer

VOCABULARY

The following section includes both familiar and obscure terms used in cooking, dining, and entertaining. In it you will find the names of beverages, foods, and dishes that you may come across as you refine your cooking and entertaining skills. Most of the terms include a description of the item, its origin, and its basic ingredients. At the end of each subsection, you will find an area marked **Notes** where you may add your own terms and definitions.

A

St. Andre cheese	See cheese.
aap-gerk	Chinese. Duck feet soup. ✎ The duck feet are sautéed in butter, then cooked with bamboo shoots, mushrooms, water chestnuts, chicken broth, sherry, and soy sauce. It is garnished with pineapple slices.
abalone	*Abulon*. Spanish American from the American Indian language of Monterrey, California. A large edible mollusk with a flat shell that is lined with mother-of-pearl. They are commercially grown in California, Mexico, Japan, and South Africa.
absinthe	A green, bitter European liqueur originally flavored with wormwood, anise, fennel, balm and hyssop.
Absolut	A name brand black currant flavored vodka.
Absolut Citron	A name brand vodka flavored with lemon, lime, and lemon peel.
achards	East Indian pickle mix made with melon, celery, bamboo, radishes, cucumbers, Indian corn, mushrooms, and nuts in spiced vinegar.
acorn squash	An autumn or winter squash that is acorn-shaped and has a rind that is dark green and ridged. The flesh is sweet and varies in color from yellow to orange.
acrid	Sharp and harsh to the taste. Bitter.
adobo	❖ Spanish. A Caribbean or Philippine spice mixture. ❖ A dish made of fish or meat that is browned in oil then marinated in an adobo sauce that is made with the spice mixture, garlic, and vinegar.
advocaat	A Dutch liqueur made with brandy and egg yolks.
adzuki bean	❖ *Adzuki*. A small, oval shaped, dark purple Asian bean. ❖ The flour made from the Adzuki bean.

agar	Malayan *agar-agar*. A gelatinous extract taken from some seaweeds and red algae. ✓ Agar gels better than the gelatin taken from animals.
aiguillettes	French. Long, thin strips of poultry breast that are cut with the grain of the meat.
aile	French. A poultry wing.
aioli	French. Garlic mayonnaise. Made of olive oil, crushed garlic, egg yolks, and lemon juice.
Alabama Slammer	A tall bar drink made with a shot each of Amaretto, Southern Comfort, and sloe gin. Sweetened lemon juice is added to the mixture and then served over ice.
à la carte	French. A menu in which the foods are priced separately.
à la grecque	French. Served Greek style, which is in a sauce made of olive oil, lemon juice, and seasonings.
à la king	Served with a white sauce, mushrooms, and bell pepper or pimiento.
à la mode	French. Topped with ice cream.
albacore	Tuna. A large marine food fish that is cut into tuna steaks and is also canned.
albuféras	Small arrak flavored cakes, topped with almonds, and baked. Frosted with rum flavored fondant.
al dente	Italian. A term that refers to the optimum doneness of pasta. Literally, it is "firm to the bite".
ale	An alcoholic beverage brewed by fermenting malt with hops. Ale resembles beer but is more full-bodied.
Alexander	A bar drink made with gin, crème de cacao, light cream, and a sprinkle of nutmeg.
allasch	A rectified kümmel flavored with caraway.
Alligator	A tall bar drink made with Midori liqueur and orange juice over ice.
Alligator Bite	A bar drink made with whisky, Madder liqueur, and sweet and sour mix. It is served over ice and garnished with a slice of lime.
allspice	See allspice under **Spices**.
almond	A nut that is the kernel of a peach-like fruit that grows on a tree from the rose family.
amandine	French. Made or served with almonds.

amaretti	Italian macaroons made with bitter almonds.
amaretto	Italian. An almond flavored liqueur.
American cheese	See cheese.
amer picon	A French bitters.
ancho chili	A ripe, dried pablano chili that is reddish-brown in color.
anchovy	Spanish. A small herring-like Mediterranean fish that is used in sauces, as appetizers, and as a garnish.
angel food cake	A white sponge cake made with flour, sugar, and egg whites.
angelica	A sweet, white or light amber fortified wine that is produced in California.
Angostura	A Venezuelan bitter, formulated in 1824 by Dr. J. Siegert to use as a tonic. Named after the town of Angostura, it is made from the bitter bark of the Casparia tree, herbs, and spices.
anise	See anise under **Herbs**.
anisette	French. A colorless sweet liqueur flavored with aniseed and coriander.
antipasto	Italian. ❖ Hors d'oeuvres. ❖ Hors d'oeuvres served as an entree.
aperitif	A small before-dinner alcoholic drink used to increase the appetite.
apfelstrudel	German. Apple strudel. Thin layers of pastry filled with apple slices, raisins, and nuts.
appareil	French. A culinary term for a prepared mixture.
apple	A red, yellow, or green skinned fruit with a crisp, sweet or tart, cream-colored flesh, and a core containing hard, dark brown seeds. The apple tree is from the rose family.
apple butter	A thick, sweet, spicy, spread made of stewed apples.
applejack	A brandy made from apple cider that is left outdoors to ferment during the winter.
apple martini	A bar drink made in a martini glass and containing vodka or gin, Apple Pucker, and sweet and sour mix.
Apple Pucker	A brand name apple liqueur.

applesauce	Stewed apples that have been pureed and sometimes sweetened.
apricot	The small orange-colored fruit, native to North China, with a sweet-tangy flavor similar to that of peaches and plums which are from the same family. Apricots grow in temperate areas.
apricot brandy	*Abricotine* (French). A sweet, brandy-based cordial made with fresh or dried apricots.
apry aquavit	❖ A very sweet apricot-flavored liqueur with a grape brandy base. ❖ A rectified colorless Scandinavian spirit distilled from potatoes or grain and flavored with caraway seeds.
arborio rice	An Italian short grain rice.
armagnac	A French brandy distilled from grapes grown in Armagnac in the Gers district of France.
aromatics	*Aromates* (French). Ingredients that lend fragrance and flavor to a dish. Herbs, spices, and pungent vegetables such as onions and garlic fall into this category. Aromatics may be used in the process of cooking and/or added to an already cooked dish.
arrack	Indian. *Arack. Arrak.* A strong spirit distilled from rice and molasses or toddy originally made in India. ✓ Batavia arrack is distilled from molasses and rice in Indonesia.
arrowroot	A starch used to thicken sauces and pie fillings. Arrowroot comes from the roots of the tropical American Maranta plant and is used in the same way as corn starch. ✓ It must be removed from the heat when it starts boiling. Arrowroot thickens like corn starch but it is less sticky and more transparent.
arroz con pollo	A Spanish/Mexican dish made of chicken, rice, onions, and spices.
artichoke	The green bud-shaped flowering head of an herb plant that is used as a vegetable. Native to Europe and Africa, also grown in America.
arugula	A European herb from the mustard family the leaves of which are used in salads.
Asiago	See cheese.
asparagus	The young, multiple shoots sprouting from the roots of the asparagus plant. Asparagus stalks are green and have small scale-like leaves.
aspic	A savory gelatin made with stock. Can be used as a garnish or to make a meat, fish or vegetable mold.
assaisonner	French. To season.

atjar ketimun	A Jewish cucumber relish made with cucumbers, onions, garlic, ginger, turmeric, sugar, vinegar, and almonds.
au gratin	French. Topped with grated cheese or bread crumbs and browned under a broiler.
au kirsch	French. Made with kirsch or kirsch syrup.
au poivre	French. Served with a large amount of coarsely ground black pepper.
autumn squash	A squash that matures in the fall, such as acorn, butternut, or hubbard.
avocado	The pear-shaped, dark green to purple-skinned fruit of a tropical tree. The flesh is bright green to yellow in color with a texture that is soft and smooth, and has a sweet, nut-like flavor. It has one dark brown bone (seed) in the center.

Notes:

_____
_____
_____
_____
_____
_____
_____
_____
_____

 B

B-52	A tall bar drink made with Kahlúa, Bailey's Irish Cream, and Grand Marnier.
baba	French. Rum cake. A rich French cake that is soaked in a sugar syrup and rum mixture.
baba ghanoush	An Arabic savory spread made with roasted eggplant, olive oil, lemon juice, sesame paste, and garlic.
Baby Margarita	A signature non-alcoholic drink made with one part Rose's lime juice, three parts club soda or 7-Up, served over crushed ice in a Margarita glass with a salted rim. Garnished with a lime slice.
Baccardi	A name brand Puerto Rican rum.
bacon	Meat that is taken from the side of a hog, then smoked, and salt-cured.
bagasse	French. *Megasse*. The dry residue left after processing grapes, sugarcane, or olives.

Bailey's	Bailey's Irish Cream. A popular brand name creamy liqueur made with cream, eggs, chocolate, and Irish whiskey.
bain marie	French. A hot water bath used to keep soups and sauces warm.
bake	To cook in the oven.
baking powder	A leavening agent that is made of starch or flour, a sodium carbonate, and an acid.
baking soda	Sodium bicarbonate which is used as a leavening agent. ✓ Baking soda can be used to put out small grease fires. Keep some next to the stove.
balm	See balm under **Herbs**.
bamboo shoot	Malayan. The immature stems of the bamboo plant that are used in Asian dishes.
banana	The long tapering tropical fruit with a yellow peeling and soft, sweet, edible flesh. Grows upside down in long hanging bunches from a tree of the Musaceae family.
bannock	❖ Britain. A large round, unleavened bread made of oatmeal and wheat barley. ❖ New England. A thin cornbread cake baked on a grill.
barack palinka	A hot, dry Hungarian brandy distilled from ripe apricots.
barbecue	*Barbacoa*. Mexican/southwestern U.S. origin. To broil on a rack or a revolving spit over hot coals or open flames. Usually done outdoors.
barbel	A freshwater fish native to Europe.
bard	Barder. *Lardone* (French). To cover lean meats with slices of bacon before cooking.
barley	Barley-corn. A cereal grass or the grain from the barley plant.
barley-bree	Scottish whisky or malt liquor.
barley malt	Barley that has been ground into a coarse meal and dried over a peat fire.
baron of beef	A double loin of beef cut in one whole piece so that the legs and loins are still joined at the backbone.
baron d'agneau	French. Baron of Lamb. The saddle and legs of lamb are in one piece. (This term is sometimes mistakenly used when referring to mutton in general.)
barquettes	Pastry boats filled with salpicon puree or salads. Served hot or cold.
basic stock	*Fond* (French). See stock.
basil	See basil under **Herbs**.

basmati rice	Hindi. An aromatic long-grain rice.
bass	An edible spiny finned marine or freshwater fish.
baste	To ladle hot liquid over food as it roasts with a large spoon or basting bulb.
batata	Spanish. A Latin American sweet potato. Also called boniato.
Batida de Coco	A Brazilian coconut liqueur with a cachaca or rum base.
bauernschmaus	An Austrian dish made of sauerkraut with dumplings, potatoes, smoked pork, sausage, and boiled bacon.
bauerwurst	German. See cure.
Bavarian cream	*Bavarois* (French). A sweet custard or fruit puree combined with gelatin and whipped cream.
bay leaves	See bay leaves under **Herbs**.
bean	The seed or immature legume pod of an upright or climbing bean plant. Beans come in many different varieties including the following:

	butter bean	A green shell bean such as the Lima, sieva or wax bean.
	green bean	Snap bean. The green pods of a kidney bean.
	kidney bean	A large reddish-brown seed of a kidney bean plant.
	lima bean	The large green or buff-colored seed of the tall, bushy Lima bean plant native to South America.
	navy bean	The white seed of a kidney bean plant.
	pinto bean	*Frijole* (Spanish). A speckled kidney bean grown mainly in the southwestern U.S.

bean curd	*Dofu* (Chinese). *Tofu* (Japanese). A high protein, low calorie, and no cholesterol food that is made from soybean milk. It has a smooth texture and bland flavor that mixes well with other foods. Usually used in stir-fried dishes and soups.
béarnaise	A sauce made of egg yolks, butter, shallots, wine, vinegar, and seasoning.
beat	To stir vigorously in a circular motion with a whisk or an electric mixer, to make the mixture lighter.
béchamel	French. A white sauce made with melted butter, flour, milk, and seasoning.
beef	The meat of a mature domestic cow, usually a steer (a castrated young bull).
beet	❖ A plant that is used as a vegetable with small, round, dark red edible roots, the leaves are also edible. ❖ Sugar beet. The bulbous, white root of a beet plant that is a large source of sugar.

bell pepper	Sweet pepper. A large, bell-shaped, thick-skinned, fleshy, mild pepper. Bell peppers may be green, red, orange, or yellow.
beluga	Beluga caviar. A black Russian caviar taken from a large, white sturgeon (beluga) native to the Black and Caspian Seas and their tributaries.
Benedictine	A pale green herb trademark cordial that is sweet and very aromatic. Named for the monks of the Benedictine order in Fecamp, Normandy.
Berkshire soup	An English soup made of onions, tomatoes, beaten eggs, flour, cream, and spices. Garnished with parsley and croutons.
Bermuda onion	A large, cream colored, sweet onion.
berner platte	A Swiss dish made of sauerkraut or green beans with boiled beef and bacon, sausage, pork chops, ham, and tongue.
berry	❖ The small pulpy edible fruit of varying shapes and colors, such as blueberries, blackberries, and strawberries. Also the pulpy fruit of various plants such as grapes and tomatoes. ❖ The roe of a fish or lobster.
beurre	French. Butter.
beurrecks	Turkish cheese sticks.
bias	Diagonal. To cut diagonally across the grain.
bienenstich	German. A honey and almond cake.
bierwurst	*Beerwurst.* A dark, German cooked sausage with a pungent garlic flavor, usually used as a sandwich meat.
bind	To bring dry ingredients together into one clump by moistening with a liquid.
Bird's nests	*Nids de hirondelles* (French). Gelatinous nests of a South Asian swift that make their nests on the cliff walls along the coast and on cave walls. The nests are made from seaweed, and are protein rich with a delicate flavor. They swell up when soaked in water and are used for bird's nest soup.
biscochito	Spanish. A sugar cookie made with anise seed and coated on one side with a mixture of sugar and cinnamon before baking.
biscotti	*Biscotta.* A crisp Italian cookie flavored with anise seed and almonds.
biscuit	❖ A kind of short bread baked in small individual cakes and raised with baking powder or baking soda. ❖ British. A cookie or sweet cracker.

bisque	French. A thick creamy shellfish, game, or vegetable soup that is thickened with rice and was originally made with biscuits or bread crusts.
bistro	❖ French. A small bar or tavern. Usually serves food.
bitok	*Bitki*. A small, round, flat Russian dumpling of raw or cooked meat. Fried and served with a sauce.
bitters	An alcoholic solution made from bitter, aromatic plants. Used in preparing mixed drinks and as a stomach tonic.
black bean	❖ A Latin American kidney bean. ❖ A black soybean used in Asian cooking.
blackberry	The purplish-black, sweet, succulent, many seeded fruit that grows on a thorny bramble.
blackberry brandy	A spiced blackberry cordial with a brandy base.
blackberry liqueur	A blackberry-flavored liqueur made from blackberry brandy with a small amount of red wine.
Black Cow	A beverage made with vanilla ice cream, root beer, chocolate syrup; topped with whipped cream and a maraschino cherry.
black pudding	Blood sausage. Blood pudding (Irish). A dark British sausage made of a pig casing filled with pig's blood and chopped fried onions. Blanched, broiled or fried and served with mashed potatoes.
Black Russian	A short bar drink made with vodka and Kahlúa over ice.
blancher	French. To blanche. To scald by immersing in boiling water. 🥄 Place meat to be whitened or strong flavored vegetables in cold water and bring to a boil. Drain and cook. 🥄 Place green vegetables in boiling water and cook for one minute or in a steamer for 5 minutes. This method will stop oxidation and can be used for most vegetables that are to be frozen for future use.
blanqette	French. Chicken, rabbit, lamb, veal or seafood stew in a rich sauce of cooking stock to which milk or cream and egg yolks are added, e.g., Blanquette of Lobster.
Blavod	A brand name premium quality black vodka from the U. K. The black color is natural and comes from the Burmese herb, black catcheu. Even though this vodka is black, it has neither smell nor taste and will not stain clothing.
blend	❖ To stir all of the ingredients together until the mixture is smooth. ❖ A combination of herbs, spices and seeds.

blinis	Russian pancakes.
blintzes	Rolls made of small pancakes or crepes filled with cottage cheese, egg yolks, sugar and orange or lemon zest.
bloater	A salted and smoked herring or mackerel.
blood sausage	See black pudding.
Bloody Mary	A tall bar drink made with tomato juice or Bloody Mary mix, Worcestershire sauce, Tabasco, salt, pepper, the juice of six lemons or limes, celery salt, and one shot of vodka. Garnished with a celery stick.
blueberry	The dark blue skinned berry with sweet, sometimes tart, succulent flesh, and many tiny seeds. Blueberries grow on a variety of bushes distributed throughout Europe, the U.S., and Canada.
blue cheese	See cheese.
Blue Curaçao	A brand name, blue colored, sweet triple-sec.
Blue Hawaiian	A tall bar drink made with pineapple juice, Parrot Bay coconut liqueur, and Blue Curaçao. Served over ice.
bock	A dark, rich, heavy German beer.
boil	To heat water or another liquid until it bubbles or reaches the boiling point.
Boiler Maker	A bar drink made by dropping a shot of whisky into a mug of beer.
boiling point	The boiling point is the temperature at which a liquid boils. ✓ The boiling point of water is 212 degrees F (100 degrees C) at sea level.
bok choy	A Chinese lettuce with long white stems and green leaves.
boletus	A large mushroom with a yellow or brown rounded cap and a white stem.
Bologna	Italian. *Boulogne*. Boloney. A precooked and sliced seasoned sausage made of beef and pork, sometimes turkey. Named for Bologna, Italy, but its original name was *mortadella*.
Bombay ducks	*Bummaloe* fish imported from India. They come canned, smoked or dried, and are served with curry dishes.
bombe	A frozen French dessert in the form of a ball made with layers of different favored ice creams.
bonbon	French. A chocolate covered fondant filled candy.

bone	To remove the bones from meat, fish or poultry.
boonekamp	A bitters containing cloves, fennel, coriander, gentian, liquorice, curaçao orange peels and other flavors.
bordelaise	A sauce made with thickened stock, red wine, and shallots.
bouchée	❖ A French sauce made with a white sauce base with added white wine, cream, and lemon juice. ❖ An appetizer made of small puff pastry patties filled with purees or ragouts and topped with a mushroom instead of pastry.
bouillabaisse	French. A fish stew usually made with lobster, shrimp, bass, mussels, and clams. Seasoned with onions, leeks, garlic, tomatoes, fennel, bay leaves, and oil.
bouillon	❖ French. Broth. ❖ See bouillon under **Spices**.
boule	A term used to describe the shape of a bread that is formed by hand and baked without a pan.
bouquet garni	French. A bunch of herbs or vegetables that are tied together or placed in a permeable container and used to flavor stews and sauces. ✎ Parsley, thyme and bay leaves usually make up this bouquet. Sometimes, leeks, celery, and carrots are used in the same way. Remove the bouquet before serving.
bourbon whiskey	Whiskey made from fermented grain mash and must be 51% corn.
bourride	French. A fish stew thickened with egg yolks and flavored with garlic. Similar to *bouillabaisse*.
boysenberry	The large berry that grows on a bramble. Boysenberries are a hybrid cross between a blackberry and a raspberry, and have a flavor that is similar to a raspberry.
braciola	French. ❖ A thin slice of meat wrapped around a seasoned filling and cooked in wine. ❖ A slice of meat roasted over hot coals.
braise	To brown meat or other food in oil then transfer to another pan which is covered and cooked slowly in a small amount of liquid. ✓ Braising will usually tenderize the toughest meats.
bran	The outer seed coverings of cereal grains that are broken up and separated from the flour by sifting.

brandy	❖ An alcoholic beverage distilled from wine or fermented fruit juice, usually from grapes. ❖ To mix, flavor, blend, or preserve with brandy.
bratwurst	A German fresh pork sausage made for frying, grilling, or cooking.
breadfruit	A round, greenish-brown, seedless, tropical fruit with a white, meaty pulp that has the same color and texture of bread when it is baked. Breadfruit is from the mulberry family and is high in starch. It is native to the Malay Archipelago but grows throughout the South Pacific.
bread pudding	A dessert made of bread slices or pieces, corn or maple syrup, and milk, then sprinkled with cinnamon and baked.
bree	*Brie. Broo*. A Scottish broth or brew.
brew	❖ To prepare a beverage by infusion in hot water such as in making hot tea or coffee. ❖ To prepare beer or ale through boiling, steeping, and fermentation. ❖ A brewed beverage such as beer or ale.
Brewer's yeast	A yeast that is a primary source of B-complex vitamins and is also used in brewing beer.
brick cheese	See cheese.
brider	To truss poultry.
Brie	See cheese.
brill	A European food fish.
brine	A salt water solution used for preserving meats and for pickling.
broche	French. *A la broche*. Cooked on a spit over hot coals or an open fire.
brochette	French. *En brochette*.
broccoli	A vegetable from the cauliflower family with green or purple florets arranged into a compact head.
broccoli rabe	Broccoli raab. A relative of the turnip with many stalks and leaves, and yellow flowers.
broil	To cook meat, fish or poultry directly over the flame of a grill or under a gas or electric range broiler.
brose	A Scottish stew made by adding meal, such as cornmeal, to a boiling liquid.

brown	To cook at high heat in fat or under a broiler until golden brown.
brown Betty	A baked pudding made of apples, bread crumbs, and spices.
Brown Cow	A bar drink made with Kahlúa and milk, served in a flute, and garnished with a sprinkle of nutmeg.
brunoise	French. ❖ Vegetables that are cut into very small cubes. ❖ A garnish for *consommé*.
Brussels sprouts	A variety of cabbage that has numerous small heads along the stalk that are used as vegetable.
bulgar	Turkish. Parched crushed wheat.
Bullfrog	A party punch made with lemonade and vodka.
Bundt pan	Funnel cake pan. A deep, round baking pan with an opening in the center. Used for baking cakes and as a gelatin mold.
Bourbon	An American corn-based whisky. Originally made in the 1700's in Bourbon County, Kentucky.
burgoo	❖ A thick, highly spiced meat and vegetable soup usually served at picnics. ❖ A picnic or barbecue where burgoo is served. ❖ Hardtack cooked with molasses. ❖ Thick cooked oatmeal porridge or mush.
Burgundy	❖ A red or white unblended wine originally made in Burgundy, France. ❖ A blended red wine made in locales throughout the world.
burritos	Mexican/southwestern U.S. A flour tortilla rolled around a filling of beans and cheese or beans, cheese, lettuce, tomatoes, and sour cream.
butter	❖ A solid produced by churning cream so that it emulsifies. Butter is used as a spread, a frying medium, and as a cooking and baking ingredient. The following is a list of those most commonly referred to:

	beurre blanc	Butter sauce made with butter, white wine or vinegar, fish stock and chopped shallots. Served with boiled or poached fish.
	beurre noir	Deeply browned butter with reduced vinegar or lemon juice. Sometimes parsley or capers are added for flavor. Served with fish or brains.
	beurre manie	Kneaded butter or butter paste. A mixture of two parts butter and one part flour is worked into a paste then whisked, one small piece at a time, into an almost cooked liquid or broth. Used as a thickener.

The Ultimate Kitchen Consultant

clarified butter	Butter that has been heated until foaming, skimmed, then cooled and the milky liquid drained off.
green butter	Butter sautéed with chives and parsley.

❖ A buttery food or creamy spread, i.e., peanut butter.

buttermilk
❖ The liquid remaining after butter has been churned.
❖ Sweet milk to which a beneficial bacteria has been added. Compare with yogurt.

butter paste   *Beurre manie* (French). See butter.

butternut squash   A tapered autumn or winter squash with a cream-colored rind and orange flesh.

buttery
❖ Has the flavor and consistency of butter.
❖ A pantry.
❖ A wine or liquor cellar.

button mushroom   A widely cultivated and commonly used small white mushroom with round caps, gills on the underside of the cap, and a mild flavor.

Notes:
_____
_____
_____
_____
_____
_____
_____
_____
_____

C

cabaret
❖ Nightclub.
❖ Liquor store.

cabbage   A European green, leafy garden vegetable with a single short stem and a compact head. Red cabbage, native to China, has dark purple leaves.

cabbage turnip   A member of the cabbage family with roots that grow above ground and tops that can be used like spinach.

cabernet   Cabernet sauvignon. A dry red French wine made from one variety of a black grape.

cacao	Spanish. Cocoa. Cacao or cocoa beans are the lightly fermented beans of a South American evergreen tree that are used to make cocoa, chocolate, and cocoa butter.
cachaca	*Caxaca. Caxa. Chacha.* A rum flavored Brazilian liqueur made from the juice of unrefined sugar cane.
cadgerie	*Kedgeree.* An Anglo-Indian dish made of alternating layers of cod, cooked rice, egg slices, and cooked onions. Topped with a curried cream sauce.
café	❖ A small, casual establishment that generally serves coffee and meals. ❖ Spanish. Coffee.
café au lait	Coffee with milk. Sometimes half coffee and half hot milk.
café noir	❖ Black coffee. Coffee without cream or sugar. ❖ *Demitasse* (French).
cake flour	A pre-sifted flour made especially for making cakes.
calabaza	❖ Spanish. A pumpkin or squash. ❖ A pumpkin that is native to Latin and South America.
calabasita	❖ Spanish. An immature pumpkin that is used as a squash. A *calabasita* has a richer flavor than a zucchini or other squash. ❖ Mexican/southwestern U. S. A dish made with sautéed calabasitas, corn, and green chili. Sometimes made in a white sauce or gravy.
calamata olives	*Kalamata* olives. Purplish-black Greek olives.
calomandin	A small, tart Philippine orange similar to a kumquat.
Calvados	One of the finest dry apple brandies. Made in Calvados, France. Distilled in a pot still and aged in oak barrels for up to 40 years. Used in dessert dishes and in mixed drinks.
Camembert	See cheese.
Canadian bacon	Bacon that is taken from the loin and contains very little fat. It is usually cut into round slices.
Canadian whiskey	Traditionally spelled *whiskey* not *whisky*. Rye whiskeys are made from rye and bourbon whiskey is made from corn. All of which contain some barley and malt.
canapé	French. ❖ A small slice of bread cut into various shapes and served plain, toasted or fried. Canapés are topped with a spread and garnished, then served as an appetizer or cocktail snack. ❖ Crackers topped with cheese or caviar.

cannoli	Italian. A tube shaped pastry filled with seasoned and sweetened ricotta cheese, then deep fried.
cannelloni	Italian. A tubular form of ravioli filled with chopped braised beef, calf's brain, chopped spinach, and bound together with thick demi-glace. It is placed in a greased baking dish, covered with thick veal gravy, topped with grated Parmesan, and sprinkled with oil; then baked until the cheese melts.
canola oil	Europe. Rapeseed oil. An oil made from the seeds of the rape plant, a member of the mustard family. Compared to other edible oils, canola or rapeseed oil has the lowest level of saturated fat. Canola oil is also used in margarine, soap, and lamp oil.
cantaloupe	A muskmelon with a rind that has a rough mesh-like texture and dark orange, sweet, succulent flesh. The center is hollow and contains a fibrous, viscous network of seeds.
capers	See capers under **Spices**.
Cappuccino	Italian. Capuchin. Espresso coffee that is mixed with frothed hot milk or cream, and sometimes sprinkled with cinnamon. The name is taken from the color of the Capuchin's habit.
Captain Morgan	A name brand spiced rum.
carambola	Star fruit. A yellow tropical fruit with five ridges that run from top to bottom and a cross section that resembles a star.
caramel	❖ Browned melted sugar. ❖ A chewy, stretchy candy made from melting and browning sugar then adding butter and evaporated milk.
caramel color	Burnt sugar that is dissolved in water and used as a coloring liquid.
caramelize	❖ To dissolve sugar in water and boil without stirring until it is a rich tan color. ❖ To sprinkle sugar over a dessert and broil until it forms a thin caramel layer.
caramote	See scampi.
caraway seed	See caraway seed under Herbs.
Car Bomb	A tall bar drink made with Guinnes beer and Bailey's.
carbonade	French. ❖ To cook over coals. ❖ A beef stew made with beer.
carbonado	Spanish. A cut of meat that is scored before grilling.

cardamon	See cardamon under **Herbs**.
cardoon	*Cardon* (French). *Karde, Kardi* (German). ❖ A plant from the thistle family that is grown for the root which is sliced and and boiled, then served as a salad. Also, the stalks of the inner leaves which are cut and boiled, then used as a vegetable. ❖ Parmesan and breadcrumbs sprinkled with oil and baked until golden.
Caribbean	A tall bar drink made with light rum, triple sec, fruit juice, and Rose's grenadine syrup. Served over crushed ice.
Caribbean Punch	A party punch made with champagne, Cointreau, brandy, carbonated water, sugar, lemon and lime slices, pineapple chunks, and garnished with strawberries.
carrot	The long, orange colored, tapering edible root of the carrot plant used as a fresh or cooked vegetable.
casaba	*Cassaba*. A variety of muskmelon, originally from western Turkey, with a yellow rind and sweet white flesh.
casein	A phosphoprotein that is produced when milk is curdled by rennet. Casein is the essential ingredient in cheese.
cashew	A kidney-shaped nut with a lightly sweet, beige kernel that is edible after roasting.
cassata	An Italian ice pudding made with a mold of ice cream or pudding filled with a mixture of diced fruit, macaroons, and nuts bound together with mousse.
casserole	French. ❖ Dutch oven or stew pan. ❖ Stews made of meat, poultry, fish or game, and vegetables that are cooked in liquid either on the stove or in the oven.
cassis	French. Black currant.
cassolette	French. A small container or pot used for preparing and serving one portion of a dish.
catfish	A freshwater, smooth-skinned, bottom-dwelling, carnivorous food fish with whisker-like barbs which enable them to find their prey in muddy waters.
caudle	A drink made with warm wine or ale that has been mixed with bread or gruel, eggs, sugar, and spices. Originally made for invalids.
cauliflower	A variety of cabbage cultivated for its large, white, and compact immature flower.
caviar	The salted and processed gold, red, or black roe that is harvested from large fish, such as sturgeon or shad. Usually considered a delicacy.

cayenne	See cayenne under **Spices**.
celeriac	Celery root. An edible bulbous root.
celery	A European herb that is cultivated for its long, green, ribbed stalk for use as a fresh or cooked vegetable.
celery seed	See celery seed under **Spices**.
certosa	An Italian liqueur similar to Chartreuse. Comes in different colors and flavors.
cervelat	French. *Cervelas*. A beef and pork smoked sausage.
Chablis	❖ A sharp, dry white or Burgundy wine originally made in Chablis, France.
chafing dish	A fondue or heat-resistant dish which is used to make fondue in and to keep the fondue or other food warm at the table.
Champagne	❖ A white sparkling wine originally made in the old province of Champagne, France. ❖ A white effervescent wine made in other parts of the world with the same characteristics as French champagne.
champignon	French. A field mushroom.
chantarelle	French. *Chanterelle, griolle. Pfifferling, eierschwamm* (German). An edible deep yellow-colored, fragrant, mild flavored mushroom. Both wild and domestically grown.
chapone	French. A crust of bread rubbed with a clove of garlic and placed in the bottom of a green salad to give it a light hint of garlic. Discard the *chapone* after tossing the salad in dressing.
char	To scorch or lightly burn.
charbroil	To cook by broiling on a rack above hot coals.
chard	Swiss chard. A type of beet with large leaves and succulent stalks. Chard is cooked similar to spinach.
charger	A large flat dish or base plate that is placed under the dinner plate. Usually used for formal dinners or to protect table cloths from becoming stained.
charlotte	A dessert made by lining a mold with ladyfingers or bread slices, then filling it with fruit, whipped cream, or custard.
Chartreuse	❖ A brand name yellow or green French liqueur made of herbs and spices originally made by the Carthusian monks at the La Grand Chartreuse monastery.

❖ A dish made of fish or game and vegetables.

chayotte Spanish. A widely cultivated pear-shaped West Indian vine fruit, also known as mirliton. Chayotte is used as a vegetable or in salads.

cheddar See cheese.

cheese The curdled milk that has been separated from the whey with rennet, shaped into different forms, and aged appropriately. Cheese comes from the milk of various domestic animals such as cows, goats, and sheep. There are many varieties of cheese including the following:

American	A process cheese made from American cheddar.
St. Andre	A rich, triple-cream, mild cheese.
Asiago	A hard yellow Italian cheese with a nutty flavor.
blue cheese	A white cheese with veins of green-blue mold.
brick cheese	A Wisconsin cheese named for the process used to squeeze the whey from the curds of the cheese by weighing down the slab of cheese with bricks. Brick cheese is a pale yellow, semi-soft, brick shaped cheese with a mild pungent flavor. Has a flavor similar to Limburger when fully ripened.
Brie	A soft ripened cheese originally made in the district of Brie, France. It has a white rind and light yellow center.
Camembert	A soft cheese originally made in Normandy, France. The outside rind is thin and grayish white, and the inside is yellow.
cheddar	A white, yellow, or orange smooth cheese with a flavor that sharpens with age.
chevre	A French cheese directly translated from the word *goat*. A pungent, mild, creamy to semi-solid goat cheese that comes in a variety of shapes and is usually coated in vegetable ash. Sometimes coated with herbs or pepper.
Colby	A moist, mild cheese similar to cheddar made in Colby, Wisconsin.
cottage cheese	Dutch cheese. Pot cheese. *Smearcase*. A very mild (almost flavorless) soft white cheese made from the curds of skim milk.
cream cheese	*Mascapone* (Italian). A soft, mild, unripened cheese made from whole sweet milk that has been fortified with cream.
Edam	A yellow Dutch cheese formed into flat wheels and encased in red wax.
Emmenthal	*Emmenthaler. Emmental. Emmentaler.* Switzerland's oldest cheese with a natural light brown rind and golden center that is permeated with large holes, and has a mild nutty flavor. Emmentaler is named for the Emmental Valley and is exported in giant wheels weighing between 150 and 220 pounds.
feta	A hard, crumbly Greek cheese made from goat or sheep's milk and cured in brine.
Gjetost	A Norwegian lightly sweet, golden-brown cheese made from a blend of cow's and goat's whey. Compare with mysost.

	gouda	A mild Dutch cheese comparable to Edam but with a higher fat content.
	Gruyere	A hard nutty flavored Swiss cheese with small holes or a process cheese made with Gruyere.
	Limburger	A soft German cheese with an orangish-brown rind and an overwhelmingly pungent aroma and flavor.
	longhorn	A hard mild cheese such as cheddar or Colby.
	Monterrey Jack	A semi-soft, whole milk cheese with a high moisture content.
	Montrachet	A mild goat cheese.
	mozzarella	A moist white unsalted and unripened Italian cheese with a mild flavor and a smooth rubbery texture.
	Muenster	A soft French cheese that ranges from mild to sharp in flavor.
	Mysost	*Primost*. A golden-brown, lightly sweet, spreadable Scandinavian cheese made with cow's milk
	Parmesan	A very dry, hard, sharp Italian cheese that is sold in wedges but is usually grated and used as a topping for spaghetti, pizza, etc.
	process cheese	Processed. A blend of several different batches of cheese.
	ricotta	A white, unripened Italian cheese similar to cottage cheese.
	Romano	A hard, sharp Italian cheese that is usually grated.
	Roquefort	French. A trade mark strong blue cheese made from goat's milk.
	Swiss	See *Emmenthal* cheese.

cheese cloth A thin gauzy cloth used for straining foods such as cheese.

chemiser French. To line a mold with jelly, ice cream, forcemeat, etc.

cherries jubilee A dessert made of cherries in a thick sauce of red currant jelly and arrowroot. It is served in a small silver bowl, with Kirsch poured over the top and lit on fire.

cherry The yellow to red, or near black fruit of the cherry tree. The cherry has a small pit and a small pit and smooth outer skin, and its flavor ranges from tart to very sweet depending on the variety.

cherry brandy A sweet cordial with a brandy base and made from the juice of ripe cherries.

cherry liqueur A rich heavy liqueur made of wild cherries in a base of brandy.

chervil See chervil under **Herbs**.

chestnut The reddish-brown edible nut of the chestnut tree.
  ✎ To cook chestnuts, pierce the skin and immerse briefly in hot fat, boiling water, or bake on a baking sheet sprinkled with water. The skin will come off easily.

chevre See cheese.

57 Chevy A tall bar drink made with Southern Comfort, amaretto, rum, orange juice, and grenadine.

Chianti	❖ Chianti or white Chianti. A dry red or white wine originally made in the Monti Chianti region of Italy. ❖ A wine similar to an Italian Chianti that is made in other regions of the world.
chicken chang	Chicken pieces browned in butter and cooked in white wine with green onions.
chicken essence	*Essence de volaille* (French). Chicken trimmings or stock with mushrooms which has been boiled down for about an hour or until very strong.
chicken Senegalese	Republic of Senegal. A chilled soup made of chicken broth, curry powder, lemon juice, grated apple or mango, sugar, and cream. Garnished with toasted grated coconut and served chilled.
chicory	❖ Endive. Escarole. A lettuce-like herb with narrow curly leaves that is used in salads and as a vegetable. ❖ The roasted and ground roots of the chicory plant that are used as a coffee additive or replacement.
chick pea	See garbanzos.
chiffon	French. Adding whipped egg whites or gelatin to create a light delicate texture to a dish.
chiffonade	French. ❖ Shredded leafy vegetables or salads. ❖ Chopped or finely cut vegetables that are used as a garnish.
chili	Spanish. A hot or sweet pepper that is usually green, yellow or red.
chili con carne	Mexican/southwestern U.S. A spicy stew made with minced or ground chili, chopped or ground meat, and pinto beans.
chili con queso	Mexican/southwestern U.S. A creamy dip made of melted cheese, milk, and green chili peppers.
chili powder	See chili powder under **Spices**.
chili relleno	Mexican/southwestern U.S. A fresh green chili pod stuffed with cheese, dipped in beaten eggs, and fried until golden brown on each side.
chill	To cool in the refrigerator or over ice.
Chinese cabbage	An elongated cabbage with long light green or pale yellow leaves.
Chinese sausage	*Lop chong*. A smoke cured, highly seasoned, lightly sweet, hard, dry pork sausage that is high in fat. Used in stir-fried dishes.
chives	See chives under **Herbs**.

chocolate	Spanish. ❖ Ground, roasted cacao (cocoa) beans. ❖ A food made from ground, roasted cacao beans. ❖ A beverage made with chocolate and hot water. ❖ A candy bar made with chocolate.
Chocolate Cake	A tall bar drink make with vanilla vodka, Frangelico, crème de cacao, and coconut liqueur over ice.
chop	Cut into small pieces with a sharp knife.
chop suey	A Chinese dish made with water chestnuts, bean sprouts, and bamboo shoots, and beef, chicken, or fish. Usually served over rice and seasoned with soy sauce.
chorizo	A highly seasoned Spanish pork sausage that is flavored with chili powder and garlic.
chow chow	❖ Chinese preserves made with ginger, fruit, and peelings in heavy syrup. ❖ A relish made with chopped pickles in a mustard sauce.
chowder	A thick fish or shellfish soup made in a seasoned milk base with tender chunks of chunks of fish and vegetables. Chowder can also be made with meat and vegetables.
chow gai pan	An Asian dish made with water chestnuts, bean sprouts, bamboo shoots, mushrooms, walnuts and snow peas. Served with rice and garnished with walnuts.
chow mein	A Chinese seasoned stew made with shredded or diced meat, vegetables, and mushrooms. Chow mein is usually served over fried noodles.
chutney	A Hindu condiment made of fruit, vinegar, sugar, and spices.
chworost	A Russian dessert pastry made of flour, eggs, sugar and rum then twisted into ropes and fried in butter. Sprinkled with sugar and cinnamon and served cold.
cider	❖ The juice of a fruit, usually apples and sometimes cherries. ❖ Fermented, sometimes carbonated, apple or cherry juice.
ciernikis	Russian cheese cakes made with cottage cheese mixed with flour, eggs, and melted butter. Seasoned with salt, pepper, and nutmeg, and shaped into round flat cakes poached in boiling water and served in a timbale dish covered with melted butter.
cimier	French. A saddle of venison.
cinnamon	See cinnamon under **Spices**.
ciseler	French. To score, incise or make small cuts on both sides of small fish so that the heat will get through faster.
citral	French. A lemon flavoring.

citron	❖ A lemon-like fruit that is larger and less acidic than a lemon. ❖ A watermelon that is small and hard fleshed. ❖ A confection made from the rind of either fruit.
clam	An edible bivalve marine or freshwater mollusk that lives in sand or mud.
claret	❖ A red table wine from the region around Bordeaux, France. ❖ Any red table wine similar to it.
clarify	A method for removing sediment from used fat by melting the fat. ✎ Boil two parts fat with one part water, strain, cool. and scrape away sediment. ✎ To clarify butter, the butter is heated until foaming, skimmed, then cooled and the milky liquid is drained off. ✎ To make cold stock clear, whisk two egg whites into it while bringing it to a boil. Cool and strain.
cloche	French. A concave silver or glass cover to keep food warm, i.e., pheasant under glass.
cloves	See cloves under **Spices**.
cobbler	❖ A deep dish pie with a thick upper crust and no lower crust. ❖ An alcoholic beverage made with various wines and spirits, served over shaved ice. Garnished with citrus slices or a sprig of mint.
cockscombs	*Crêtes de Coq* (French). Cockscombs are the tufts that grow on the heads of adult male fowl and are considered a delicacy. ✎ Place in cold water and heat gently until the thin skin is easily removed. Keep in cold water until ready to cook. Cook in lemon juice and butter or in white stock (*fond blanc*) made from boiling veal with herbs, onions, and mushroom stems then simmer for three hours. Strain off stock.
cocktail	❖ A flavored drink made with wine or distilled liquor on shaved ice. Sometimes garnished with a ribbon of lemon peel. ❖ An appetizer.
coconut	The fruit of the coconut palm tree. The nut is held inside a fibrous husk and contains a sweet, white, fibrous, edible meat and a milky juice (sometimes mistakenly called coconut milk).
coconut milk	Coconut milk is made by simmering water with coconut meat, which is then strained and used as an ingredient in dishes and mixed drinks. ✓ Do not confuse coconut milk with coconut juice. See coconut.
cocotte	French. A small individual dish or earthenware pot, or a large oval pot with a lid for cooking *poulet* or *poussin en cocotte*.
cod	A north Atlantic, bottom-dwelling food fish usually found from Norway to Newfoundland.

coffee	Arabic. *Quhwa*.
❖ A tropical plant from the madder family, the beans of which are roasted and ground, then brewed into a beverage.
❖ A cup of coffee.
coffee cake	A sweet, spiced bread made with nuts and fruit.
cognac	A blend of French brandies distilled from white wine. The are several different classifications according to taste:

E-extra or special	F-fine	M-mellow	O-old
P-pale	S-superior	V-very	X-extra.

For example: V.O.P. means that the cognac is very old and pale.

Cointreau	French. A brand name white, high quality orange liqueur made with curaçao orange peel and other oranges.
colander	A perforated plastic or metal bowl used to drain food.
Colby	See cheese.
cold duck	A bubbly drink made from a combination of Champagne and sparkling Burgundy.
Collins	❖ A tall glass used for bar drinks.
❖ A bar drink made with one tablespoon corn syrup, the juice of one medium lemon, and 2 jiggers of liquor. Stirred together with a few ice cubes and filled with carbonated water.
Colorado Bulldog	A short bar drink made with vodka, Kahlúa, half and half, and a splash of Coke.
Compari	An Italian bitter with an sharp, bittersweet flavor. Created in 1860 by Gaspare Campari in Milan and used as an aperitif.
compote	❖ A fruit topping made by placing fresh, frozen, or dried fruit into a boiling sugar syrup and simmering for about fifteen minutes.
❖ A glass, porcelain or metal bowl used to serve compote, fruits, nuts, or desserts.
concasser	A French term used in vegetable preservation meaning to chop or shred coarsely.
conch	A large spiral, cone-shaped marine mollusk.
condensed	Cooked down to a concentrate, e.g., canned soups or milk.
condensed milk	Sweetened evaporated milk with a consistency resembling that of a glaze.
condiment	A substance that is used to heighten the flavor and aroma of food, i.e., spice, seasoning, sauce, or relish.

condimenter	French. To season with condiments.
consistency	Used to describe the thickness of a mixture, e.g., batter, dough, or sauce.
consommé	A well-seasoned clear French soup made from concentrated, clarified meat stock and served hot or cold.
Continental	A bar tall drink made with light rum, crème de menthe, lime juice, and powdered sugar. Garnished with a lemon peel.
cool	To bring to room temperature.
cooler	A drink of carbonated water, ginger ale, or soda served over ice in a tall glass.
copocollo	Italian. A seasoned pork butt basted with hot red peppers and served with antipasto.
coquille Jacqueline	French. A baked seafood dish made with scallops in an avocado sauce.
coquille St. Jacques	A scallop that is found on both sides of the Atlantic.
coq au vin	French. Chicken cooked in red wine.
cordial	❖ Liqueur. ❖ A small aperitif of liqueur served before dinner.
cordial medoc	A liqueur made of orange curaçao, cognac, and crème de cacao.
Cordon Bleu	An elite culinary school for professional chefs.
coriander	See coriander under **Spices**.
corn	Maize. The kernels of a tall grain grass native to America that grow in rows on the long tapered ears that grow along the stalk and are encased in husks. Corn is eaten on or off the cob as a vegetable. Corn comes in several varieties and colors.
corn dog	A frankfurter or wiener on a stick, dipped in batter, and deep fried.
cornpone	Southern/central U.S. Bread made with cornmeal, water, and salt, but usually without milk and eggs.
cornstarch	A very fine corn flour used as a thickener and in making corn syrup.
Cosmopolitan	A bar drink made with vodka, triple sec, Roses's sweetened lime juice, cranberry juice and garnished with a lime wedge. Served in a Margarita glass.
cottage cheese	See cheese.

cotto salami	A salami studded with black peppercorns.
coulibiac	A Russian fish pie.
courgette	French. *Courge*. A small squash such as a zucchini.
couronne	French. *En couronne*. To arrange food in a serving dish in the shape of a crown.
court bouillon	A stock made for poaching fish or veal and for use in sauces. It is made with root vegetables, white wine or vinegar, herbs, and seasonings.
cowpea	A black-eyed pea.
crab	A marine arthropod crustacean. Crabs usually have a large body and spider-like legs.
crab apple	A small, sour apple that grows on wild or cultivated trees.
cracknel	Crackling. A hard, brittle biscuit.
cranberry	A red acidic berry from the heath family with a smooth outer skin, very tart flesh, and many tiny seeds.
crawfish	Spiny lobster. A marine crustacean native to the Mediterranean, Adriatic Sea, and the southern coasts of Ireland and England. The crawfish is from the lobster family but smaller, and without claws, long feelers, or strong spines.
crayfish	Crawdad. A freshwater crustacean found in European and American lakes and rivers.
cream	❖ The part of the milk that contains 18-40% milk fat and is pale yellow in color. Cream rises to the top of raw or pasteurized milk and is the part of the milk that is used to make real butter. ❖ To beat to the consistency of thick cream or until it is soft enough to almost drop from a spoon.
cream cheese	See cheese.
créme	The name of a number of very sweet French liqueurs made with fruit or other flavoring. Some of the most popular crèmes are:

d'ananas	pineapple	**de menthe**	peppermint	**de vanille**	vanilla
de bananes	banana	**de moka**	coffee	**de cacao**	chocolate
de noyau	cherries	**de cassis**	black currant	**de prunelle**	sloe plums

crème de cassis	A deep red, sweet, black currant French liqueur that was first produced in the 16th century by French monks as a cure for snake bites, jaundice, and fatigue.
cremini	A large, tan, fleshy mushroom similar to the portobello but smaller and less mature.

crepe	A very thin French pancake made of eggs and flour. Crepes can be sweet or savory.
crepine	French. See pig's caul.
crepinette	A flat round sausage made of poultry or game forcemeat that is encased in pig's caul, brushed with butter, rolled in breadcrumbs, and grilled. Usually served with a complimentary sauce.
Crocodile	A tall bar drink made with Madori, Bacardi Limon, and Sprite. Served over ice.
croquette	French. A savory mixture shaped into balls and chilled before dipping in beaten egg yolks, rolled in bread crumbs and deep fried. Made with boiled eggs, mashed potatoes, fish, meat, or mincemeat and held together with thick béchamel sauce.
crusta	A bar drink that is served in a glass with a rim that has been moistened with lemon juice and dipped in sugar.
croustade	French. *Crosta*. A crisp shell made of toast or puffed pastry in which food is served.
croute	French. Small round or other shape of bread, not pastry dough, lightly toasted or fried and topped with a savory mixture.
crouton	French. Small cubes of toasted or crisply fried bread for garnishing soups, salads, and other dishes.
crumble	To break up with the fingers or by hand.
crumpet	English. A thin leavened cake cooked on a griddle, then toasted and buttered.
crush	To make into crumbs by hand, with a rolling pin, etc.
crustacean	Shellfish such as a crab or lobster.
Cuba Libre	A tall bar drink made with light rum, the juice of half a lime, and Coke.
cucumber	The elongated, green skinned fruit of the gourd family native to northwest India. Eaten fresh in salads or alone. Often pickled or cooked.
cuisine	The style or quality of preparing food, or the food itself.
culinary	Pertaining to the kitchen or cooking.
cumin	See cumin under **Spices**.
Curaçao	❖ An orange-flavored liqueur originally made in Holland from green curaçao oranges, sugar, and brandy. ❖ A clear, orange liqueur flavored with the bitter peel of curaçao oranges, and

sold as blue, green, yellow, or white (clear) Curaçao. The colors have the same orange flavor and are used to add color to mixed drinks. Made in three grades: sec, double sec, and triple sec.

curd   The thick casein-rich part of coagulated milk.

curdle   When a smooth substance separates into its solid and liquid parts because of heat or acid, e.g., milk separates into curds and whey when it is mixed with rennet and then scalded. Another example, using milk, is when milk curdles upon exposure to heat and light or when it is outdated.

cure   To preserve foods. There are several methods of curing foods:

cold smoking	(70-90 degrees F, 21-32 degrees C)
hot smoking	(100-190 degrees F, 38-88 degrees C)
pickling	(preserved in a vinegar mixture)
salting	(generously salted and packed, sometimes dried)

curn   Scottish. Grain.

curry   See curry under **Spices**.
- A Hindu dish or sauce seasoned with several pungent spices.
- A dish or food seasoned with curry powder.

custard   A sweet, cooked mixture of eggs and milk, similar to pudding.

Custom Berries   A bar drink made with Frangelico, Royal Chambord, amaretto, and half and half.

cut in   To mix shortening or other fat into flour so that it forms course crumbs.

cuttlefish   A marine ten armed mollusk similar to squid and prepared in the same way.

czipetke   Hungarian. Noodle dough, dried, torn by hand, and boiled in salt water.

Notes:

D

D's Almond Joy	A signature bar drink made with Parrot Bay or Malibu and Patron Silver Tequila. The rim of the glass is dipped in chocolate syrup, then in coconut flakes, and garnished with coconut flakes.
daiquiri	A Cuban cocktail made with light rum, sweetened lime juice, and powdered sugar.
dampfnudeln	A German dessert made with yeast dough formed into small balls and placed in a greased baking pan with a small amount of milk. Brushed with egg and baked then served hot with a vanilla sauce.
dandelion	A common, spring herb that grows in sandy, grassy areas. Its bright yellow flower is used as an herb, a garnish, and to make dandelion wine. The leaves are blanched and used in salads.
Danish	A pastry made of sweet, raised dough.
Danziger Goldwasser	A rectified spirit flavored with cinnamon, coriander, herbs, and spices. It is lightly sweetened and contains a large quantity of gold leaf fragments. Originally distilled in Danzig (Gdansk), Germany.
dariole	French. Small beaker mold.
darne	French. Middle section of a fish, e.g., salmon or tuna.
date	A pulpy, brown fruit that is filled with tiny seeds. Dates grow on a Middle Eastern palm tree and are be eaten fresh or dried.
daube	❖ French. Braising. *Boeuf en daube* is braised beef. ❖ A braised meat stew with vegetables, herbs, and spices.
Debonnet	A French wine based aperitif. Available in rouge or blanc.
decoct	To extract the flavor of by boiling.
deglaze	French. To heat de-fatted stock and wine together with the sediment left in a roasting pan to make a gravy or sauce.
degorger	French. To remove strong flavors and impurities before cooking. ✎ Soak meat such as game meat in cold salted water for a few hours before cooking. ✎ Sprinkle sliced vegetables with salt, place a cutting board over them and leave them for an hour or so. Rinse them off and pat dry on a paper towel.
degraiser	French. To de-grease or skim fat off of soups, sauces, or stocks.
degraissis	French. The fat skimmed off of stocks, soups, etc. It is clarified and used for cooking vegetables.

demitasse	French. A small cup of black coffee also refers to the cup it is served in.
desosser	French. See bone.
devil	To marinate or apply a seasoned or spiced paste to meat, fish or poultry before broiling, frying, or serving, e.g., deviled eggs.
Devil's food cake	A rich mahogany colored chocolate cake.
dew-peen	Asian. Squid.
dice	To cut meat, fruits, vegetables or breads into small cubes.
dill	See dill under **Herbs**.
dim sum	Chinese appetizer such as steamed or fried dumplings, cooked chicken pieces, or rice balls.
dissolve	To melt a solid substance by mixing with a liquid, sometimes over heat.
dofu	Chinese tofu.
double boiler	A pan that consists of two pans fitted together so that water can be boiled in the bottom part and the upper part can be used to make delicate sauces or to steam vegetables.
double de mouton	French. *Double d'agneau*. Two legs of mutton or lamb in one solid piece.
dough	A mixture of flour or meal with liquid and fat that is kneaded together and used for making bread and pastry.
doughnut	A small ring-shaped pastry made from cake or yeast dough and deep-fried.
doux	French. Very sweet. A term usually used to describe the sweetness of a Champagne.
drain	Pour off liquid.
drambui	A liqueur made from Scotch whisky, honey, herbs, and spices.
Dreamsicle	A short bar drink made with Bailey's and orange juice.
dress	To prepare for cooking or for the table.
dresser	French. To dress, arrange or garnish.
dressing	*Farce* (French). Forcemeat or stuffing. ✎ Made with savory ingredients, such as fish, game, ground meat, ground pork,

or poultry mixed with breadcrumbs or rice, vegetables, nuts, and spices. Bound together with eggs, milk or sauce. Stuffing is used to flavor meat, poultry and fish. It can be stuffed into cavities or served alone between portions. Stuffing can also be baked or fried separately and served with the main dish.

drunk chicken
- Shanghai, China. A chicken dish in which the chicken is marinated in wine for about 24 hours, steam cooked, and served cold.
- A whole chicken that is cooked on a barbecue grill or over an open fire with a full, open can of beer in the body cavity. The chicken is cooked standing on end so as not to spill the beer.

dry duxelles
Duxelles seche.(French).Chopped onions and shallots sweated in one part oil and one part butter. Used for sauces and so forth.
- Add ten times the amount of finely chopped and pressed out mushroom stems, and simmer until dry. Add chopped parsley, salt and pepper. When cold, put in pot and cover with greased paper.

dumpling
- A small ball of dough dropped into stew or soup, e.g., chicken and dumplings.
- A serving size piece of pastry filled with fruit, sugar and spices then baked or steamed, e.g., apple dumpling.

Dutch oven
- A heavy pot with a tight fitting concave lid.
- A cast iron kettle with a tight lid that is used for baking over an open fire.
- A brick oven in which the cooking is done by the pre-heated walls.

duxelles
French. *Duxelles pour de legumes farcis. Duxelles* for stuffing or garnishing vegetables. *Duxelles* is made primarily of finely chopped and dried mushrooms.
- Dry *duxelles* are boiled in white wine until the wine is completely reduced. Add *demi-glace* (refined brown gravy) with tomato, some crushed garlic and breadcrumbs then simmer until thick enough to stuff vegetables.

Notes:
_____
_____
_____
_____
_____
_____
_____
_____
_____
_____

E

eau de vie de marc   A spirit distilled from the grape skins that have already been crushed to make wine.

Edam	See cheese.
egg drop soup	A Mandarin dish made by stirring beaten eggs into boiling pork broth.
egg fu yung	A Chinese omelet prepared in a wok with mushrooms, bean sprouts, bamboo shoots, carrots, and onions.
eggnog	A traditional Christmas holiday beverage made with eggs, sugar, milk, cream, and rum or rum flavoring.
eggplant	The purplish-black, pear-shaped fruit of the nightshade family that is used as a vegetable. Native to Asia.
egg roll	A Chinese appetizer made of minced vegetables and sometimes pieces of meat, shrimp or chicken rolled into a thin egg dough and deep fried.
egg roll skins	Chinese. Very thin pastry sheets made with high-gluten flour and water.
egg whites	The whites of the eggs that have been separated from the yolks. ✎ Egg whites must be completely yolk-free so that they whisk easily. Whisk slowly, gradually increasing speed as whites begin to stiffen. Add a pinch of salt for a savory dish or a teaspoon of granulated sugar for meringue to keep the egg whites from turning.
eiswein	German. Ice wine. A sweet wine made from grapes that froze while still on the vine.
elderberry	A red or black berry similar to a cherry in appearance and flavor.
Emmenthal	See cheese.
emulsified	Made into a mixture that does not naturally blend, i.e., cream in milk, or water or vinegar in oil.
enchilada	Mexican/southwestern U.S. ❖ Seasoned with chili. ❖ A dish made with layers of fried corn tortillas, beans, cheese, onions, lettuce, and tomatoes. Usually served with red or green chili and sometimes topped with a fried egg. ❖ A rolled corn tortilla stuffed with seasoned meat, chicken, or cheese and covered with chili sauce.
endive	See chicory.
entree	French. Appetizer. The main course of a meal in the United States.
enzian	A spirit distilled from the roots of gentian that grows in the Alps and the Pyrenees. Originally made in Germany and Switzerland.

escalope	French. *Callop*. Scallop. A very thin piece of meat or chicken that has been pounded flat.
escargot	French. A snail used for food.
escarole	See chicory.
Espagnole	A basic brown sauce.
espresso	❖ Italian. Coffee brewed by forcing steam through finely ground, darkly roasted coffee beans. ❖ A cup of espresso.
essence	*Fumet* (French). An aromatic base made by reducing or boiling down a solution into a concentrate, e.g., seasoned chicken broth with white wine.
etamine	French. A loosely woven light cotton cloth that is used for straining fluids, such as soups and sauces.
etouffée	A Cajun stew made of shellfish or chicken that is served over rice.
étuver	French. To stew or steam in very little liquid.
evaporated milk	Unsweetened canned milk that has been partially evaporated or boiled down to a concentrate.

Notes:

_____
_____
_____
_____
_____
_____
_____
_____

F

faht-choy	Chinese. A hair seaweed with a tart flavor.
fairy ring mushroom	A small mushroom with a reddish cap and buff-colored stem and gills.
fajardo	Spanish. Meat pie.

fajita	Mexican/southwestern U.S. Marinated and grilled meat, chicken, or shrimp rolled up in a flour tortilla.
falafel	Arabic. Spiced vegetables that are ground up and made into patties.
farce	French. Forcemeat, stuffing, or dressing. Usually served between courses. See dressing.
farcir	French. To stuff or fill.
farina	Starch. A finely ground meal or flour made from cereal grains, nuts, potatoes, or corn and used as a breakfast cereal or in puddings.
fennel seed	See fennel seed under **Herbs**.
fenugreek	See fenugreek under **Spices**.
feta	See cheese.
fête	A festival or celebration. Usually held outdoors.
fettuccine	Fettuccini. An Italian pasta that is shaped like long, narrow ribbons.
fettuccine Alfredo	Fettuccine in Alfredo sauce. ❧ Alfredo sauce is made with butter, Parmesan cheese, cream, and seasonings.
file	French. Young sassafras leaves crushed into a powder and used as a thickener in soups or stews.
filet	French. Fillet. ❖ A strip or slice of boneless meat or fish. ❖ To slice, bone or make into a fillet or fillets.
filet de boeuf	French. ❖ Fillet of beef. ❖ Tenderloin. The undercut of the loin which is the tenderest cut of beef. The meat is carefully trimmed, larded, and roasted. Served whole or pan roasted, hot or cold.
filet mignon	French. *Filet Mignon de boeuf*. Meat taken from the end of the tenderloin that is too thin to be used for fillet steaks. ❧ These are the two most common ways to prepare a filet mignon: Cut into a triangular shape, lightly flatten, season, dip in melted butter and breadcrumbs and grill slowly. Cut and season the filet in the same way as above, then wrap it in a strip of bacon and grill slowly.
fillet	A term used in regards to citrus fruit. The flesh is cut out in sections without skin, pith or pips.

fines herbes	French. *Aux fines herbes*. A blend of herbs used in French cuisine usually in egg dishes, sauces, and soups. ✎ Chervil, tarragon, chives and sometimes parsley are chopped and mixed together to create this herbal blend.
fish essence	Fish bones and heads, sliced onions, mushroom pieces, and parsley stalks sweated in butter. ✎ Cover with half fish stock and half white wine, cook slowly for 20 minutes, then add a little strained lemon juice.
five-spice powder	Chinese. A blend of star anise, cinnamon, cloves, fennel, and Szechuan peppercorns.
fizz	A well-mixed, frappéed alcoholic drink strained into a glass then fizzed with a stream of club soda or seltzer water. Serve while foaming.
flapjack	See pancake.
flambée	French. Fire or blaze.
flamber	French. ❖ To flame or ignite. ❖ A method used to singe poultry, game or other dish by pouring warm brandy, spirits, or sherry over the food in the pan and setting it ablaze. Continue to cook or serve flaming.
Flaming Dr. Pepper	A bar drink made with amaretto, beer, and 151 rum floated on top. Light the rum on fire and serve. Tastes like Dr. Pepper (a name brand carbonated beverage).
flan	French. ❖ A shallow pastry shell that has been molded in a metal ring and set on a baking sheet. ❖ Flan also refers to a baked custard. ❖ Mexican. A caramel baked custard flavored with Angostura bitters.
fleurons	French puff pastry rolled out into a thin sheet, cut into crescent shapes, brushed with egg and baked in a hot oven. *Fleurons* are used as a garnish.
flip	An alcoholic beverage made with a wine or liquor shaken with sugar or syrup, and a whole beaten egg. Strained into a glass and served with a sprinkle of nutmeg.
float	❖ Ice cream soda. A drink made with soda pop, usually root beer or cola, and a scoop of ice cream. ❖ A bartending term meaning to pour a liquid so that it is separated from the other liquids. A liquid is floated if it lies on top of the other liquids in a glass or floated to the bottom if it is poured so that it rests at the very bottom of the glass.
Florentine	Italian. Named for the city of Florence, it refers to a dish served, dressed, or garnished with spinach.

flounder	A marine food fish from the flatfish family.
flummery	A cold rice or semolina pudding served with a cold fruit sauce or sabayon.
flute	To decoratively seal the rim of a pastry crust or pie shell. Can be done with a fluting tool or with the finger tips.
fold	To very gently mix a light substance with a heavy one so that the mixture remains light. Folding is done by lifting from beneath and folding over.
fond	French. Basic stock.
fondant	French. A soft creamy candy.
fondue	French. ❖ A party dish made with Gruyere or Emmenthal cheese, white wine, and kirsch. It is served in a chafing dish or casserole on a burner to keep it warm. Use fondue forks to dip cubes of bread into the melted cheese dish. ❖ Chocolate or white chocolate may be used to make dessert fondues. In this case, fruits and cake squares are dunked into the rich chocolate dip. ❖ A chafing dish in which fondue is made and served.
fondue Bourguignonne	French. Cubes of raw beef fillet that are dunked a pan of hot oil then dipped in an assortment of spiced sauces in separate dishes. Named for the region of Burgundy.
fool	A fruit puree blended with thick, whipped cream.
forbidden fruit	A sweet citrus liqueur made of brandy, West Indian grapefruit, and other flavorings.
forcemeat	❖ *Farce* (French). Stuffing. ❖ Meat, poultry, fish or game that has been pounded in a mortar or finely ground then rubbed through a sieve, mixed with eggs or *panade*, and highly seasoned. May be used for stuffing or served alone. ❖ *Mousseline* forcemeat is made of meat, fish, poultry, or game that is rubbed through a sieve and seasoned. Egg whites are mixed in to form a paste then cream is whipped into it until the mixture is light and fluffy. ✓ *Mousseline* forcemeat must be very light. Test it by dropping a small spoonful in boiling hot water. It should float to the top.
fortified wine	A wine that has had grape brandy added to it to make it stronger.
fozy	Too ripe, usually referring to fruit.
Frangelico	A brand name hazelnut liqueur.
frankfurter	German. Hot dog. A smoke, seasoned, cooked sausage. Usually made of pork, beef, chicken, turkey, or a mixture of meats. May be encased or skinless.

frappé	French. ❖ A chilled or partially frozen fruit drink. ❖ An extra thick milk shake. ❖ An icy drink made by pouring liqueur into a glass of shaved ice.
frapper	French. To chill.
freeze	To chill below the freezing point of water which is 32 degrees F (0 degrees C). ✓ Freezers should be kept at 0 degrees F (-18 degrees C).
French	❖ To cut vegetables into thin strips before cooking. ❖ To prepare chops or rib roasts by trimming the meat from the ends of the bones.
French fried	Cooked by deep-frying until crisp.
fricadeller	French. Ground raw or cooked meat shaped into small balls and fried.
fricassée	French. ❖ Reheated, cooked chicken in white sauce. ❖ Stew of white meat, poultry, fish or vegetables. Usually served with a white veloute sauce.
fried bananas	Deep south, U.S. Sliced bananas dipped in egg, rolled in bread crumbs, and fried until golden brown. Usually served with ham, pork, or chicken.
frijoles refritos	Pre-cooked pinto beans that are mashed and seasoned with chili peppers, onions, and garlic then lightly fried.
fritter	Cooked meat, raw or cooked vegetables, or fresh fruit dipped in batter then deep fried in oil.
friture	French. ❖ Fritter or any fried food. ❖ Frying fat. ❖ The food that is fried in fat.
frosting	Icing. A sweet, creamy mixture that is spread on baked goods, e.g., cakes or cookies.
froth	❖ Mousse. ❖ A very light and fluffy cold or hot forcemeat preparation. ❖ A light ice or cream.
fruit bread	A sweet bread made with stewed pears, lemon peel, figs, raisins, hazelnuts, almonds, cinnamon, cloves, nutmeg, sugar, and rum. Wrapped in bread dough and baked.
fruit cake	A rich cake made with nuts, spices, dried currants, raisins, golden raisins, and candied orange and lemon rinds that have been steeped in rum.

fry	To cook in hot oil usually over direct heat. The following are the most common ways to fry foods:
dry fry	To cook over high heat in oil that barely covers the base of a frying pan.
shallow fry	To cook eggs, fish, breaded chops briskly without burning in a 1/2 inch (1.2 cm) layer of oil.
deep fry	To immerse and fry food in oil. Deep fat frying is meant to seal in the food's flavor and should be very hot. Drain deep-fried food on paper towels or on a wire rack.
✓	Strain used oil and keep covered for future use. Oil used for frying fish should be saved and used for fish only.
frying pan	Skillet. A wide shallow metal pan with a handle. Used for frying food.
fumet	French. ❖ Essence. A well-reduced fish or game stock. ❖ The bouquet of a wine. ❖ Aroma or scent.
fu yung	Chinese. A sauce made by thickening chicken stock with cornstarch and seasoning with soy sauce and anise.
Fuzzy Navel	A bar drink made with peach schnapps and orange juice.

Notes:

_____
_____
_____
_____
_____
_____
_____
_____
_____
_____
_____

G

galantine	French. A boneless type of meatloaf in skin that is served chilled. Galantine is garnished and set with gelatin.
Galliano	*Liquore Galliano*. A sweet, yellow, herbal Italian liqueur.
gamay	❖ A grape that is French in origin. ❖ A dry red table wine that is made from the gamay grape. This same grape is also used to make French Beaujolais.

game essence	*Essence de gibier*. Game stock. ✎ Chop game trimmings into small pieces and brown in butter with sliced onions and mushroom stems and pieces. Allow seasonings to permeate the meat, then cover with water, cook for two hours and strain.
ganache	French. A creamy chocolate mixture used as a filling or frosting.
garbanzos	Spanish. Chick peas, an Asian legume.
garlic	See garlic under **Herbs**.
garnish	To decorate creatively or to use a specific garnish, e.g., a simple sprig of parsley to add color to an omelet or a decorative arrangement of fresh herbs and lemon slices on a salmon fillet.
gateau	A large, rich cake sometimes filled with cream and frosted. Usually decorated.
gazpacho	Spanish. A spicy soup made with tomatoes, onions, peppers, cucumbers, oil, vinegar, eggs, and seasonings. Garnished with slivers of fresh tomatoes, peppers, and cucumbers. Served chilled.
gelatin	❖ *Gelato*. Viscous material collected by first boiling and then cooling down animal tissue. ❖ Unflavored powdered gelatin is used to set molds, aspics or creams. ❖ Flavored gelatins such as cherry, orange, or strawberry. ❖ A sweet or savory mold set with powdered gelatin. ❖ Dissolve in hot water then dilute with water, desired base or fruit juice.
gelfite fish	Jewish. A dish made with ground carp, pike and whitefish mixed with cracker crumbs, minced onions, and eggs, then rolled into balls. The fish balls are simmered in fish stock made from the fish heads, skin, and bones. Served with horseradish.
genever	Dutch. *Geneva*. Gin. A spirit distilled from grain and malt flavored with juniper berries and wine.
genoise	Vienna cake. An Italian sponge cake named for Genoa. Made with butter and stiffly beaten eggs.
gentian	An herb native to southern Europe. The roots and bulbs are used for flavoring vermouth and are also used as a tonic.
gherkins	Small, sweet pickles.
giblets	The liver, gizzards, neck, and heart of poultry.
gin	An aromatic alcoholic beverage distilled from various grains and flavored with juniper berries, anise, and caraway. There are two types of London gin, dry and sweet.

ginger	See ginger under **Spices**.
gingerbread	A spiced cake made with flour, eggs, butter, ginger, spices, and molasses.
gjetost	See cheese.
glacé	French. ❖ Glazed or glossy. ❖ Iced, icy, frozen, or chilled. ❖ A sugar icing for cakes, donuts, cookies or candied fruit. ❖ A jam or fruit glaze for coating desserts and cakes. ❖ *Glacé de viande* or meat glaze. This glaze is made by reducing meat stock to the consistency of jelly or by dissolving gelatin in meat stock. It is then used to coat cold meats, glaze cooked meats, or for strengthening soups and sauces. This glaze may also be made of fish, chicken, or game stock.
glacer	French. ❖ To glaze. ❖ To freeze. ❖ To make shiny with a mixture of eggs, water and sugar, or milk. ❖ To rapidly brown dishes covered with a heavily buttered sauce in a hot oven. ❖ To glaze meat by basting it often with its own fat or to brush meat with liquid meat glaze. ❖ To glaze cakes or pastries with strained apricot or red current jam, or with icing.
glacier	A person who makes ice cream or a pastry cook who specializes in making ice cream.
glogg	A Scandinavian Christmas punch made with hot spiced wine and liquor.
gnocchi	Italian dumplings made of semolina flour, cream puff paste, and potatoes, then mixed or served with grated cheese.
goblet	❖ A bowl-shaped drinking vessel with a stem and without handles. ❖ A glass with a base and stem used for festive occasions.
Golden Delicious	An American grown apple with yellow skin that is lightly spattered with tiny brown speckles and five peaks on the bottom end.
Goldschlager	A name brand schnapps liqueur with a strong cinnamon flavor and 24 karat gold flakes.
gooseberry	The round, green, tart fruit of a prickly shrub from the currant family. Native to Southern Europe and North Africa.
götterspeise	German. Chantilly cream mixed with grated chocolate and pumpernickel.
Gouda	See cheese.

goulash	Hungarian. *Gulyáshús. Gulyás*. A highly seasoned Hungarian stew made with beef, veal, or lamb and seasoned with onions, vegetables, and paprika. Also known as Hungarian goulash.
Gramolata	Italian. *Granite* (French). An iced beverage similar to sorbet and served as a party drink. It is made from a light fruit syrup that has been frozen.
granada	Spanish. Pomegranate.
granadila	Spanish. An oblong shaped, pomegranate-like tropical fruit that is native to Central and South America. Used as a dessert.
granita	An Italian course textured iced dessert made from fruit.
Granny Smith	A green skinned Australian apple with crisp white flesh and a tart flavor.
granola	A breakfast cereal or snack mixture made of rolled oats, raisins, coconut, and nuts.
Grand Marnier	An orange flavored, high quality French brandy based liqueur.
grapefruit	A large yellow to yellowish-pink berry with a thick bitter rind, containing several sections of tart, juicy pulp. Grapefruits belong to the citrus family.
grappa	An Italian spirit similar to the French eau-de-vie-de-marc.
Grasshopper	An alcoholic beverage comprised of half peppermint liqueur and half crème de cacao.
grate	To scrape into small pieces by rubbing a hard food, like cheese or raw vegetables on a grater.
gratin	❖ *Au Gratin, Gratine* (French). Pertaining to food covered in breadcrumbs, grated cheese, butter, or sauce and cooked in the oven. ❖ Browning food under a broiler. ❖ Forcemeat *Au Gratin. Farce au gratin*. ✎ Forcemeat made of equal amounts of bacon, veal, veal liver, butter, mushroom stems and pieces, truffle peels, egg yolks, seasoning, Madeira, and reduced *demi-glac*e. Dice and sauté liver, veal, and bacon beforehand.
grease	❖ Rendered animal fat. ❖ To coat with a thin, even layer of butter, margarine, oil, or shortening.
green butter	See butter.
green tea	Tea that is light in color because the leaves were not completely fermented before they were roasted.
green vegetable color	Food coloring made from green vegetables. ✎ Wash and drain spinach well, then pound it with a meat tenderizer and squeeze

squeeze the juice out onto a clean cloth. Heat the cloth lightly in a double boiled until the green part settles to the bottom of the pan. Pour off the liquid on top, rub the green residue through a fine sieve and use as coloring.

grenadine A very sweet, ruby red, non-alcoholic, concentrated syrup made from pomegranate juice and sugar. Used for coloring and flavoring drinks and cocktails.

Gribiche A sauce made of hard-boiled egg yolks, lemon juice, vinegar, olive oil, mustard, parsley, tarragon, thyme, and capers. Served with fish.

griddle
- A flat metal pan, sometimes with a handle.
- A flat metal surface used to cook on.

grießschmarrn Austrian. *Kaiserschmarren*. Semolina cooked in milk to make a thick mush which is mixed with butter, eggs, sugar, salt, and raisins. It is cooked like pancakes which are then torn into segments, dusted with powdered sugar, and served with stewed plums.

grind To cut food into small pieces with a grinder.

gristle The tough cartilage or rigid tissue found in meats.

grouper A large, bottom-dwelling, warm water marine fish.

guacaomle Mexican. A thick sauce made of mashed avocado, lemon juice, garlic powder, and salt. Used as a topping for a variety of Mexican/southwestern U.S. dishes and served as a dip with corn tortilla chips.

gruel German. *Grütze*. *Gruau* (French). Ground grain such as wheat, barley, or oats that is boiled and served as a breakfast dish.

Gruyere See cheese.

guglhupf German. A sweet bread made of yeast, flour, milk, eggs, butter, and sugar. Mixed with raisins, lemon zest, and chopped almonds and poured into a mold that has been buttered and coated with chopped almonds and breadcrumbs. Baked and dusted with powdered sugar.

gumbo Creole. A soup thickened with okra and made with vegetables, meat, or seafood.

gurjeffski kascha Russian. Semolina cooked in sweetened milk and vanilla, then mixed with butter and butter and egg yolks. Poured into a greased baking dish with fruit macedoine that has been steeped in maraschino juice and skim milk. Covered with chopped almonds and sugar then baked. Served with an apricot sauce.

Notes:
_____
_____

H

habañero	An extremely hot, small chili pepper that resembles an orange bell pepper. Named for Havana, Cuba.
haddock	A marine food fish native to the Atlantic coasts of America and Northern Europe.
half-and-half	A mixture of equal parts milk and cream. It is 10-12% milk fat and can not be whipped.
halibut	A marine food flatfish that is native to the northern Atlantic, the North Sea, the western Baltic, and the western shores of North America. Halibut is large and bony.
halishkes	A cabbage roll dish made of ground beef, onions, and rice rolled into a cabbage leaf. Simmered in a mixture of vinegar, corn syrup, stewed tomatoes, raisins, and sugar.
hamburger	❖ Ground beef. ❖ A sandwich made of a hamburger patty in a round, split bun. Usually garnished with catsup, mustard, and mayonnaise. Often with lettuce, tomatoes, pickles and onions.
hardtack	A salt-less cracker, hard biscuit or bread.
Harrogate trifle	English. A bundt sponge cake that is cut into three or four layers. Each layer is soaked in cherry brandy syrup then coated with red currant jelly. Custard is sandwiched between each layer and the entire cake is covered with whipped cream and decorated with small macaroons.
Harvey Wallbanger	A tall bar drink made with vodka, Galliano, and orange juice.
hash	A dish made with meat and potatoes, usually with corned beef, diced potatoes, onions, and seasonings.
haute cuisine	French. An elaborate style of cooking originally tailored to and provided for the upper classes of society.
halv om halv	A bitter liqueur made from Curaçao orange peels and other flavorings.
hazelnut	A nut with a light brown shell and cream-colored, flavorful kernel.

head cheese	Brawn (English). *Fromage de tete* (French). A loaf made from the meat of an animal's head, tongue, heart, and feet by cooking it in a mold. The broth cools to form a thick jelly and the head cheese is un-molded and sliced. Usually served at room temperature as an hors d'oeuvre.
heavy cream	Heavy whipping cream. Whipping cream with a milk fat content of 36-40%.
hélianthe	A tuberous vegetable that tastes like a potato and is similar to a Jerusalem artichoke.
helvella	A flavorful cone-shaped mushroom related to the conical morel.
herbs	❖ A seed producing annual, biannual, or perennial plant that never forms a permanent woody tissue and dies down to the ground in the fall. ❖ The aromatic leaves and flowers, sometimes roots, of these plants. ❖ A plant that is used for its medicinal properties, aroma, or flavor.
hermetical sealing	The closing of a cocotte or other receptacle with bread dough or flour mixed with with water to seal in the aroma.
hering-skartoffelen	German. A casserole made with herring, potatoes, onions, butter, eggs, and milk. Topped with bread crumbs and toasted in the oven.
herring	❖ A north Pacific fish from which roe is harvested. ❖ A north Atlantic food fish that is used as sardines when it is young and is smoked or salted when it is full grown.
highball	A tall iced bar drink made with liquor and ginger ale or other soda.
himmel und erde	German. Sliced potatoes and apples cooked in a salted bouillon base and bay leaves, then pureed and served with pork.
historier	French. To decorate or embellish.
hoisin sauce	Chinese. A thick, reddish-brown sauce, with a spicy, slightly sweet flavor that is made from soybeans and spices.
hollandaise	A sauce made with egg yolks, butter, and lemon juice.
holsteiner schnitzel	A German dish made with veal escalope, topped with a fried egg, and garnished with vegetables. Served with smoked salmon, anchovies, and mussels.
hominy	White corn kernels that are used as a vegetable. ✓ Hominy is the main ingredient in posole, a Mexican/southwestern U.S. stew.
homard	French. Lobster.
homogenize	To process a product such as raw milk by using high heat and pressure to break up fat globules into tiny particles and disperse them evenly throughout the liquid.

honey	Honey is produced by honey-bees, who gather flower pollen and then regurgitate it in the form of a thick, sticky, sweet substance.
honey-comb	An edible network of hexagon-shaped wax compartments that honey-bees make and use as a nest for their offspring and for storing honey.
honeydew	A pastel green melon with a smooth rind and sweet, succulent, green flesh. The center is hollow and contains a viscous, fibrous network of seeds.
hops	The ripe, dried, scaly fruit of a perennial climbing herb that is used in brewing beer, in medicine, and as an aromatic bitter stomachic.
hors d'oeuvre	French. Hot or cold bite-size snacks served before a meal. ✓ In Europe, *hors d'oeuvres* are the first of several appetizers.
horseradish	See horseradish under **Herbs**.
hot buttered rum	A hot alcoholic drink served in a coffee cup. Made with hot water, rum, brown sugar, butter, vanilla, and spices.
hot cider	A hot drink made with apple cider, oranges, cloves, and cinnamon sticks simmered together.
hot dog	See frankfurter.
Hpnotiq	A brand name blend of French vodka, the finest still pot cognac, and natural tropical fruit juices.
Hubbard squash	A large, green autumn or winter squash.
huevos rancheros	A Mexican/southwestern U.S. egg dish made with fried eggs on a flour tortilla with pinto beans and fried potatoes, smothered in chili, and topped with cheddar cheese and chopped onions.
hure	French. Head of boar or pig. *Hure de sanglier* is wild boar's head.
hurricane	A bar drink made with one part vodka, two parts brandy, one teaspoon absinth that is shaken with ice and strained into a glass. It can also be made with light rum, dark rum, passion fruit syrup, and sweetened lime juice.

Notes:

_____
_____
_____
_____
_____
_____

I

iceberg lettuce The most widely used lettuce with light green crisp leaves, a compact head, and mild flavor.

ice wine See eiswein.

icing See frosting.

Incredible Hulk A bar drink made with Hpnotiq, cognac, pineapple juice, sour mix, and 7-Up.

infuse To steep in warm liquid so that the flavor is drawn into the liquid.

Irish coffee An alcoholic beverage made with hot coffee, Irish whiskey, brown sugar, and heavy cream. Served in a coffee cup.

Irish whiskey Traditionally spelled *whiskey* not *whisky*. A whiskey made from barley grain and as much as 40% barley malt.

Notes:

J

Jack Daniels A name brand Tennessee whisky. Made in Lynchburg, Tennessee since 1866.

Jagermeister German bitter liqueur meaning "hunt master". It is a combination of over fifty fruits, herbs, and spices.

jahnie di ciuperci Romanian. A ragout made of mushrooms, chopped fried onions, mixed with tomato puree and seasoned with salt, pepper, and dill.

jalapeño A small, green, hot, meaty Mexican chili pepper named for Jalapa, Mexico.

jalousies	A thinly rolled puff pastry, cut into wide strips, and spread with vanilla almond cream, then trellised with thin strips of puff pastry. Brushed with apricot jam, baked and sliced.
jam	A fruit spread made by boiling sugar, pectin, and whole fruit together.
Jamaican 10 Speed	A bar drink made with Parrot Bay or Malibu, Medori, banana schnapps, pineapple juice, and half and half served over ice.
jambalaya	A rice dish made primarily with fish or seafood, onions, celery, garlic, tomatoes, hot pepper sauce, and herbs. It can also be made with shellfish, chicken, or meat.
jarmus	Polish. Stewed cabbage made with white chopped cooked cabbage in a brown roux, mixed with sour cream, and garnished with braised chestnuts.
jee-choy	A tangy, purple leafed Chinese seaweed.
Jell-O	A name brand, colored, fruit-flavored gelatin mix.
Jell-O Shot	An alcoholic jelled drink made with Malibu, hot water, and watermelon Jell-O. Chilled and served set.
jelly	A fruit spread made by boiling sugar, pectin, and fruit juice together.
jerk	❖ Spanish. *Charquear. Charqui.* To cure meat by cutting into strips and drying. ❖ A special blend of spices characteristic of a certain region, culture, or cuisine, i.e., Caribbean jerk which is a combination of red and black peppers, herbs, and sweet spices.
jerky	Spanish. *Charqui.* Jerked beef. Long thinly sliced strips of meat that have been salted and seasoned, and preserved by air drying.
Jerusalem artichoke	The roots of a sunflower plant that are similar to potatoes but sweeter and starch-free.
Jewish dishes	Jewish cooking is influenced by the country or area in which the people originally lived and the traditions that have been passed on through the generations. Among these areas are Austria, Germany (Yiddish), Lithuania, the Middle-east, Poland, Romania, and Russia.
jigger	A small glass used for measuring liquor that holds about two ounces or four tablespoons of liquid. A jigger is also referred to as a shot.
John Collins	An tall bar drink made with Bourbon, lemon juice, sugar, and club soda over ice. Garnished with an orange slice and a Maraschino cherry.
johnnycake	A bread made with cornmeal.

julep	A tall iced drink made with or without liquor and sugar or syrup poured over cracked ice and garnished with mint.
julienne	French. ❖ Vegetables or other foods that are cut into fine shreds about 1/8" thick by 2" long. ❖ A clear vegetable soup to which a mixture of finely shredded cooked vegetables have been added. Similar to consommé.
Jungle Juice	An alcoholic punch made with Pisang Ambon, Gin, apricot brandy, lemon juice, and orange juice.
juniper	See juniper under **Herbs**.

Notes:

_____
_____
_____
_____
_____
_____
_____
_____
_____
_____

K

kabob	Middle Eastern. *Kebab. Kebob.* Small cuts of marinated meat cooked with vegetables and/or fruit on a skewer over an open fire or on a grill.
Kahlúa	A Mexican trademark coffee flavored liqueur.
kaiserschmarren	See grießschmarrn.
kaki	See persimmon.
kale	Cole. A leafy vegetable from the cabbage family.
Kamakazi	A short bar drink made with vodka, triple sec or Medori, and Rose's sweet lime juice. Garnished with a wedge of lemon or lime that has been dipped in course salt and then placed on the rim of the glass.
kasha	Russian. Buckwheat or a cereal made from buckwheat.
katalou	A Turkish dish made of sliced green beans, diced eggplant, green peppers, tomatoes, and okra that is cooked in oil with garlic and parsley.

kernel	The seed of a fruit or the inner part of a fruit stone, nut, or seed. Also the whole cereal seed.
key lime	A small lime that is native to and grown in the Florida Keys and the surrounding area.
kielbasa	Polish sausage. A Polish smoked sausage.
kimche	The national dish of Korea. It is a hot, spicy food made of pickled cabbage seasoned with red pepper, garlic, and ginger.
kirsch	A clear, dry, distilled German brandy made from the small, black, juicy Morello cherries native to the Black Forest in Germany, the Vosges, and Switzerland.
kishke	*Kishka*. A Slavic sausage made of meat, matzo meal, and spices then stuffed into a beef or fowl casing.
kiwi	A small Chinese fruit from the gooseberry family with brown fuzzy skin. The flesh is green, sweet, and juicy, with many tiny black seeds.
knead	To work a dough until smooth and elastic, preferably by hand.
kneaded butter	*Beurre manie* (French). See butter.
knockwurst	A thick, short, richly seasoned German sausage.
kohirabi	Cabbage turnip.
kohlroulade	German. A dish made with cabbage leaves stuffed with shredded meat.
Kool-Aid	❖ A brand name powdered drink mix. ❖ A bar drink made with vodka, Medori, and cranberry juice.
kornbranntwien	A German spirit distilled from rye, wheat, buckwheat, oats, or barley.
kosher	Hebrew. Approved or acceptable for use by Jewish law.
kosher salt	See salt.
krebinas	Chicken skins from which the fat has been rendered.
kreplach	Jewish. A stuffed dumpling similar to a wonton or ravioli.
kumquat	A small, orange-colored, Chinese berry with a soft, porous rind and tart, pulpy flesh. Kumquats belong to the citrus family and are mostly used for making preserves.
kümmel	German. A clear liqueur flavored with caraway, cumin, and anise. Originally made in Riga, Berlin, and Holland.

kwan tung chicken	An Asian rotisserie chicken.
kwas	*Kvas*. A Russian drink made by fermenting rye flour, sugar, yeast, malt, and water.

Notes:

L

la ch'ang	Chinese. A hard, spicy, cured pork sausage that is sometimes frozen.
lactose	Milk sugar.
ladyfinger	A small elongated or finger shaped sponge cake.
Lambada	A Brazilian bar drink made with cachaca, cream of coconut, cream, and maraschino cherry juice. Served over crushed ice in a decorative glass.
lard	❖ Rendered pork fat which is used for frying or as shortening. ❖ To prepare meat or poultry by sewing bacon strips into them with a larding needle.
lardons	French strips of bacon that are used to add extra fat to lean cuts of meat. See bard. ✓ Small strips of bacon, about 1/4" thick and 2" long used to give extra fat to cuts of meat that have little or none of their own to protect them from drying out during cooking. The bacon strips are larded into the meat with a larding needle.
lasagne	❖ *Lasagna* (Italian). A long, wide, flat Italian pasta. ❖ An Italian dish made by layering cooked lasagna with a tomato based meat sauce and a cheese mixture, then baked until the cheese is golden brown.
latke	A Ukranian potato cake.
leaf beet	See chard.
leaven	To raise or lighten bread with a leavening agent such as yeast, baking powder, or baking soda.

legume	The fruit or seed of a plant, such as beans or peas, that are used as a vegetable.
leek	An herb from the lily family with a flavor similar to that of onions. The leek's large leaves and stalk are used as vegetables.
lemon	An oblong berry with a yellow rind and containing several sections of very tart, juicy, pulpy fruit. The lemon is a member of the citrus family.
Lemon Drop	A short bar drink made with vodka, sour mix, sugar, and a squeeze of fresh lemon over ice. Garnished with lemon peel.
lentils	The mature gray-green to light brown seeds of a plant native to southern Europe.
lettuce	The name applied to several varieties of salad plants with succulent leaves.
liaison	French. Mixture for thickening or binding sauce, gravy or soup, e.g., roux, egg yolks, cream, or kneaded butter.
lichee	Chinese. *Lichi*. *Lichi nut*. A fruit about the size of a walnut with reddish skin, sweet white pulp, and a large seed.
light cream	Coffee or table cream. A cream that can not be whipped and usually contains 20% milk fat, but may contain 18-30% milk fat.
Lima beans	Peruvian. A flat, light green or white kidney-shaped bean.
Limburger	See cheese.
lime	A large berry with a green rind and containing several sections of very tart, juicy, pulpy fruit. Limes belong to the citrus family and are high in vitamin C.
liqueur	A sweetened alcoholic liquor with a brandy base and flavored with fruit, herbs, spices, nuts, or seeds.
liqueur d'or	A colorless, lemon-flavored imitation of Danziger Goldwasser.
Liquid Cocaine	A bar drink made with Grand Marnier, Southern Comfort, vodka, amaretto, and a splash of pineapple juice.
liquor	An alcoholic beverage made through the process of distillation instead of fermentation.
liverwurst	A German sausage made of pork liver.
lobster	*Homard, langouste* (French). *Langosta* (Spanish). *Hummer* (German). A large, ten-legged, edible, marine crustacean native to the North Atlantic and the Cape of Good Hope. The lobster has two large claws, stemmed eyes, and a long abdomen.

loin	The muscular part of an animal that includes both sides along the spine from the hipbone to the bottom of the ribs.
longan	An edible Chinese pulpy fruit.
longhorn	See cheese.
Long Island Iced Tea	A tall bar drink made with vodka, tequila, light rum, gin, and a dash of Coke. Garnished with a lemon or lime peel.
loquat	A small, yellow edible Chinese fruit with a melon-like texture and citrus flavor. Eaten fresh and used in Asian preserves.

Notes:

M

Macadamia	An Australian hard-shelled, round nut with white meat.
macaroni	Italian. A elbow shaped pasta made of flour, semolina, and farina.
macaroon	❖ An Italian cookie made from ground almonds, egg whites, and sugar. ❖ A version of this cookie made with coconut.
mace	See mace under **Spices**.
macedoine	French. Mixed vegetables or fruits, or a mixed salad.
macerate	To soak or infuse, usually fruit, in liqueur or syrup.
mackerel	A food fish that is native to the Atlantic, North Sea, Baltic, the Pacific coast of North America, and the Mediterranean.
Madeira	❖ An amber fortified Portuguese wine originally made in the Madeira Islands. ❖ A similar wine made elsewhere.

madrilene	❖ A dish made of chicken stock and fresh beets that have been boiled in sugar and vinegar. It is set with unflavored gelatin and garnished with lemon wedges and parsley. Served cold. ❖ A tomato flavored clarified beef stock.
magnum	❖ A bottle of wine or champagne that is about twice the normal size. ❖ The amount that the bottle will hold which is 1 2 liters (2 quarts).
Magyar	Hungarian. A sauce made with sautéed onions mixed with bread crumbs, poppy seeds, and seasoned with salt and pepper. Tossed with hot noodles.
mahimahi	Hawaiian, Marquesan, and Tahitian. Dolphinfish. The dolphinfish resembles a small dolphin, but is a food fish. ✓ A dolphin is a protected mammal.
Mai Tai	A bar drink made with orange, pineapple and cranberry juice, light rum, dark rum, sour mix and grenadine.
Malibu	A brand name coconut flavored Caribbean rum.
malt	❖ A germinated grain such as barley used in brewing and distilling. ❖ To combine with malt or malt extract. ❖ A single malt is a malt which is produced and bottled by one distillery and is not blended with other whiskies.
malted barley	See barley malt.
malt shake	A milk shake made with malt.
malt whiskey	A whiskey made from malted barley.
mamaliga	A cornmeal porridge.
Mandarin pancakes	Mandarin. Thin pancakes made from flour, sesame oil, salt, and water.
mandarine	A small, loose-skinned orange native to southeastern Asia.
Mandarinette	French. A tangerine flavored liqueur.
mango	Portuguese. A tropical fruit from the cashew family with a yellowish-red skin and fragrant, sweet, juicy, yellow-orange colored flesh containing one large tear-shaped stone (seed).
Manhattan	A tall bar drink made with sweet vermouth, Bourbon, Angostura, and ice cubes. The rim of the serving glass is rubbed with an orange peel. Garnished with a maraschino cherry and orange peel.

manicotti	Italian. A large, tube-shaped that is usually stuffed with cheese or meat and covered with a tomato sauce, and baked.
maraschino	A marasca cherry, sweetened and preserved in a thick syrup, and died a bright red or green. Used as a garnish and for flavoring foods and drinks, i.e., mixed drinks, ice cream sundaes, and fruit cakes.
marasquin	A liqueur distilled from marasca cherries originally grown in the region of Dalmacija, Yugoslavia.
marc de Bourgone	A spirit distilled from the skins of Burgundy grapes that have been pressed to make wine.
marc de Champagne	A spirit distilled from the skin of the grapes grown in the Champagne district which have been pressed to make wine.
marcedoin	French. ❖ A mixture of diced or sliced, cooked or raw vegetables or fruit. Served hot or cold usually with butter, dressing, or mayonnaise. ❖ A fruit marinated in syrup or liqueur.
margarine	Oleo. A vegetable oil spread that is used like butter.
Margarita	A bar drink made with tequila, triple sec, sweetened lime juice and crushed ice blended together. Served in a Margarita glass and garnished with a lime slice. For a strawberry Margarita, use strawberries frozen in sugar or fresh strawberries and sugar along with the basic ingredients. Garnished with a fresh strawberry and a lime slice.
Maragarita Glass	A wide-mouthed, shallow, bowl shaped, stemmed glass that is used to serve Margaritas in.
marinade	❖ A sauce flavored with wine, spices, and herbs in which meat or fish are soaked before cooking, to tenderize or improve flavor. ❖ A marinade can also be used for making the final sauce.
marinara	An Italian seasoned tomato sauce made with tomatoes, onions, garlic, and spices.
marinate	*Marinade* (French). To soak raw meat, game, fish or poultry in a cooked or uncooked spiced liquid mixture, made with wine, oil, herbs and vegetables, for hours or even days before cooking. This process tenderizes and flavors the meat. ✓ Always use a nonporous container, such an glass, glazed enamel or stainless steel to withstand the effects of the acid in the wine or vinegar.
marjoram	See marjoram under **Herbs**.
marmalade	Portuguese. A citrus fruit preserve made of a clear jelly with fruit pieces and rinds, such as orange marmalade.

marmelade	French. Fruit stewed and reduced to a thick, almost solid puree or butter. Used as a as a pie or flan filling.
marron	See chestnut.
marrow	❖ A variety of summer squash with smooth cream-colored to deep green skin. ❖ The soft connective tissue found in the bone cavities of animals.
Marsala	A light dry to sweet fortified white wine originally made in Marsala, Sicily.
martini	A bar drink made with one part vermouth, two parts gin, orange bitters, and Angostura. Shaken or stirred with ice, strained, and garnished with a green olive.
marzipan	French. *Marsepain*. Marchpane. An Italian candy made of blanched ground almonds or almond paste, sugar and egg whites. Marzipan is formed into various shapes and used for garnish or in decorating cakes, pies and pastry.
mascapone	An Italian cream cheese.
masquer	❖ To mask. ❖ To coat or cover any kind of hot or cold food with sauce or jelly or to cover the bottom of a dish or mold with sauce, jelly, etc.
matignon	A combination of the red part of carrots, an equal amount of onions and raw ham and a third as much celery. Cut into very small very thin slices, simmer in butter with a small bay leaf and a sprig of thyme, then *deglace* with Madeira.
matzo	Jewish. *Matzoh*. ❖ A Jewish unleavened bread that is eaten during Passover. ❖ A wafer of matzo.
matzo ball	A small dumpling made from matzo meal.
mayonnaise	A sauce made of egg yolks, mustard, lemon juice, vinegar, salt, pepper, and corn oil whipped together.
mazer	Old French. A large wooden drinking bowl.
mead	An Old English alcoholic beverage made of water, honey, malt, and yeast.
meal	The ground grain of a cereal grass, e.g., cornmeal or oatmeal.
medallion	A small, round portion of meat.
meringue	French. ❖ A light, airy mixture made by beating egg whites and sugar together. Usually used as a dessert topping on custard based pies and baked until golden brown. ❖ A dessert made with a meringue shell and filled with fruit or ice cream.
merlot	A dry red wine originally made in the Bordeaux region of France.

Metropolitan	A tall bar drink made with brandy, vermouth, a dash of bitters, and sugar.
Mexican Madras	A short bar drink made with cranberry and orange juice, gold tequila, and a dash of lime juice.
mezcal	A liquor processed similarly to tequila but not from the same region of Mexico.
Midori	A bright green, Japanese, honey-dew melon liqueur.
Midori Sour	A bar drink made with Midori and sour mix.
mie-de-pain	French. White bread with the crust removed and rubbed through a coarse sieve. ✓ Used to prepare fish, meat or poultry. Dip in beaten eggs then roll in seasoned mie-de-pain and bake until golden brown.
milk shake	A beverage made of milk, ice cream, fruit and/or flavored syrup, and egg blended together. Sometimes topped with whipped cream and a maraschino cherry.
Milky Way	A tall bar drink made with dry gin, amaretto, strawberry liqueur, strawberry syrup and pineapple juice. Garnished with pineapple, a lemon slice, and pineapple leaves.
millet	A cereal grass or its grain that is cultivated for forage but is still used in parts of Europe as a cereal.
milo	A cereal grass similar to millet or sorghum grain.
mince	To cut into very fine pieces.
mincemeat	❖ Minced meat. ❖ A mixture of minced fruits and spices, sometimes used as a pie filling.
Mind Eraser	A bar drink made with vodka, Kahlúa, and tonic water on ice.
minestrone	An Italian vegetable soup made with red kidney beans, onions, celery, cabbage, and rice or pasta.
mint julep	A bar drink made with mint, sugar, orange bitters, and gin or Bourbon in water with ice. Garnished with fruit and mint.
mirepoix	French. The basic preparation for flavoring braises and sauces. ✎ Make with carrots and an equal amount of onions and lean bacon. Add one third of the amount of largely diced celery, a sprig of thyme and a small bay leaf. Sweat these ingredients in butter to draw out the flavor. ✎ *Mirepoix bordelaise:* Carrots and an equal amount of onions, a few parsley stalks cut like *brunoise*, a pinch of thyme and powdered bay leaves are stewed slowly in butter until the moisture is completely evaporated. This is used mainly for hot lobster and other shellfish dishes.

mirliton	See chayotte.
mix	To combine ingredients.
mocha	❖ A choice, rich Arabian coffee. ❖ A mixture of cocoa and coffee.
Mojambo Punch	A party punch made with vodka, Malibu, pineapple juice, Sunny Delight, fruit punch, white grape juice, apples, and oranges. Served iced.
Mojito	A tall bar drink made with freshly ground spearmint leaves, sugar, a shot of light rum, and the juice of one lime. Served over crushed ice and garnished with a sprig of mint and a lime slice.
Mojo	A party punch made of light rum, dark rum, cherry brandy, light beer, 7-Up, and pineapple juice. Served iced.
molasses	Treacle. A thick, dark colored syrup drained off from raw cane or beet sugar during refinement.
mollusk	A soft-bodied invertebrate animal, i.e., clams, squid, and snails.
monter	French. ❖ To whip eggs or egg whites. ❖ To whip butter in a sauce, etc.
Montrachet	See cheese.
morel	A wild mushroom with a beige to brown colored cap that resembles a sponge and has a strong mushroom flavor.
Mornay	A creamy cheese sauce used in appetizers and entrees, such as fish, chicken, egg, and vegetable dishes.
mousse	French. ❖ A sweet, smooth mixture, airy but rich, made from eggs, sugar, cream with flavoring, e.g., coffee, chocolate, or fruit. ❖ Savory mousse is made from salmon, lobster, veal, chicken, cheese or vegetables, usually served chilled. ✓ Powdered gelatin may be used for setting either one.
mousseline	A sauce made by adding whipped cream or beaten egg whites to béchamel or hollandaise sauce.
mousseron	French. Fairy ring mushroom.
mozzarella	See cheese.
Mudslide	A tall bar drink made with vodka, Kahlúa, and Bailey's with crushed ice.

muenster	See cheese.
muffin	A small sweet bread made of flour, milk, butter, eggs, yeast, and salt. Baked in a muffin pan.
mulberry	A dark purple berry from the mulberry family that resembles a small cherry and grows in grape-like clusters on the mulberry tree.
mulled cider	Cider that is sweetened and spiced with cinnamon, nutmeg, cloves, and ginger, then heated and garnished with orange slices.
mulligan stew	A stew made from a variety of ingredients, depending on whatever is available.
mulligatawny	A soup made with chicken stock, onions, and carrots. Seasoned with curry, cayenne, and pepper.
muscat	❖ One of several varieties of musk-flavored grapes used in making wines and raisins. ❖ A sweet, white wine made from these grapes.
muscatel	❖ A rich, sweet French wine made from Muscat grapes which are named for their musky flavor. ❖ Wines that are similar to muscatel and that are made in the same way in other parts of the world.
mushroom	An above ground meaty fungus with a stem and a concave, convex, or flat cap that has pores or gills underneath.
mushroom essence	*Essence de chapignons* (French). The concentrate made from the short fond that mushrooms have been poached in. ✎ Mushroom essence powder: Cut dried or fresh mushrooms into slices. Dry in a warm cabinet, then pound until very fine. Dry again, sieve, and mix in a little salt and pepper. ✓ Store in tightly closed jars in a dry place for future use as flavoring in soups and sauces.
muskmelon	A sweet, pungent, edible melon that is the fruit of an Asian vine and has a rough, mesh-like rind.
mussel	❖ A small marine mollusk with a dark colored elongated tear-shaped shell. Marine mussels are found along the coastline of the United States. ❖ A freshwater mollusk whose species thrive in the rivers of the central U.S. The inner lining of their shells have a glossy finish similar to mother of pearl.
mustard	See mustard under **Spices**.
mustard dressing	A dressing made with prepared mustard, mustard seed, red or white wine vinegar, salt, and pepper.

mutton	The meat from a full-grown sheep.
mysost	See cheese.

Notes:

_____
_____
_____
_____
_____
_____
_____
_____

N

nachos	Mexican/southwestern U.S. An appetizer made of tortilla chips topped with cheese and beans and/or chili.
nalesniki	Polish. A fritter made of creamed cottage cheese, butter, eggs, and seasonings which are wrapped in very thin, unsweetened pancakes. Dipped in egg and breadcrumbs or batter then deep fried.
nan	Indian. A round, flat, unleavened bread.
Napoleon	❖ A bar drink made with gin, Curaçao, and Dubonnet rouge. ❖ A French pastry filled with cream, custard, or jelly.
navarin	A casserole made with pieces of meat, butter, sugar, wine, tomato puree, bouquet garni, and garlic. Sautéed onions and potatoes are added to the baked casserole. It is baked, once more, then garnished with fresh chopped parsley.
navy bean	See bean.
near beer	Any malt liquor that is considered non-alcoholic because it contains a small percentage of alcohol.
neat	A bartending term meaning undiluted or unmixed.
nectarine	A mutation of the peach that has smooth, hairless skin.
neep	Scottish. Turnip.
negroni	An alcoholic beverage.
Nitro	A short bar drink made with Sambucca, Goldschlagger, and brandy.

noisette	French. ❖ Small ball of rolled boneless meat, e.g., noisette of lamb. ❖ Flavored with hazelnuts. ❖ Nut-brown color, e.g., "cook butter to a noisette".
noodles	A pasta made with flour and egg yolks or whole eggs, and salt. No water is added.
Noques	*Nockerl. Nocken.* Small dumplings made of flour, eggs, milk, and butter dropped by spoon into salt water and poached.
nougat	French. A chewy candy made with honey or sugar paste and mixed with chopped nuts.
nouillettes	French. Very thin, short noodles.
nutmeg	See nutmeg under **Spices**.

Notes:

oatmeal	Rolled oats or a meal made from oats, a cereal grass.
Oatmeal Cookie	A short bar drink made with butterscotch schnapps and Bailey's.
oca	*Occa. Oxalis.* An edible root that is taken from the wood sorrel, native to South America. The oca has yellow to reddish-brown skin and white powder-like flesh.
octopus	An eight-armed cephalopod mollusk with two rows of suckers. Similar to squid.
okra	The elongated, dark green, edible pods containing many small seeds. Used as a vegetable.
old-fashioned	A bar drink made with two cubes of crushed ice, one teaspoon corn syrup, three splashes of Angostura, and 2 jigger of whisky. Stirred with a bit of lemon peel and garnished with a lemon twist and a maraschino cherry.

oleo	Margarine. The shortened form of oleomargarine.
olive	The fruit of a Mediterranean evergreen tree. Olives have a pit and can be eaten while green or ripe (black).
olive oil	Oil taken from olives. Olive oil contains no cholesterol.
omelette	French. *Omelet*. An egg dish made with beaten eggs that are cooked without stirring, then folded in half and served. An omelet may be cooked in a frying pan or on the grill. Chopped vegetables, meat, and cheese are usually mixed into the beaten eggs before cooking.
onion	See onion under **Herbs**.
oolong	A dark Chinese tea made from tea leaves that have been partially fermented before roasting.
orange	A large, round berry with an orange-colored rind and containing several sections of sweet, juicy pulp. Oranges are from the citrus family.
Orange Julius	A beverage made with orange juice, milk, water, sugar, vanilla, and ice cubes blended together.
orange pekoe	A finely sifted black tea made from the smallest and youngest tea leaves. Native to India, Ceylon, and Java.
oregano	See oregano under **Herbs**.
Oreo Cookie	A layered short bar drink made with Kahlúa, crème de cacao, and Bailey's. Topped with a splash of vodka.
Ouzo	An anise flavored Greek liqueur made from grapes, berries, and herbs. Used as an aperitif.
oxalis	See oca.

Notes:

_____
_____
_____
_____
_____
_____
_____

P

pablano chili	A large, fleshy mild green chili.
paella	A saffron flavored Spanish or Mediterranean dish made of rice with seafood or meat and vegetables.
palm shoots	The tender shoots of various palm trees that are used in salads or as vegetables.
panache	French. ❖ Mixed or multi-colored. ❖ Mixed ice, cream or jelly in a mold. ❖ Mixed fruit or vegetables.
panada	Spanish. A basic thickener for fish, meat, and vegetable molds. ✎ *Panada* is made from soaked breadcrumbs, choux (cabbage) pastry or thick béchamel sauce.
panade	French. Bread soaked in milk seasoned lightly with salt and dried by stirring continuously until the paste does not stick to the spoon. Used for fish forcemeat. ✎ *Panade a la farine*. Add butter and a pinch of salt to boiling water. Remove from heat and add sifted flour. Dry on low heat like cream puff paste. This *panade* may be used for all forcemeats. ✎ *Panade frangipane*. Stir egg yolks into flour. Add melted butter, salt, pepper, and grated nutmeg. Gradually mix in hot milk and whisk to the consistency of very thick cream. Used for fish and chicken forcemeats. ✓ All *panades* are cleared off in a pan that has been greased with butter, for future use.
pancetta	An unsmoked Itallian bacon.
pandowdy	English. A deep-dished spiced apple dessert made with sugar, molasses or syrup and covered with a rich pastry crust.
panne	French. Leaf lard. Green lard. Used primarily for forcemeat, galantines, and so forth.
papanasi cu smantana	Romanian. Fried cheese cakes served with sour cream.
papaya	An oblong shaped, yellow skinned fruit with sweet, yellow flesh containing black seeds that is native to the American tropics.
papillote	French. *En papillote*. Food that is cooked and served in a wrapper of oiled or buttered paper, or foil. The wrapping conserves juices and aromas, especially those of delicate foods.
paprikás	Hungarian. A dish made with veal or chicken baked in a sauce of chicken stock, flour, paprika, onions, sour cream, and Worcestershire. Served over noodles.

parboil	To boil until half-cooked, e.g., potatoes, before roasting.
pare	To remove a very thin layer from the surface of fruits or vegetables with a knife or peeler.
parfait	❖ A frozen dessert made with alternating layers of ice cream and syrup or fruit, and topped with whipped cream and chopped nuts. ❖ A cold dessert made with custard or pudding topped with whipped cream.
parfait glass	A tall, slender glass with a short stem and a base.
Parmesan	See cheese.
parr	Scottish. Samlet. A young salmon before its first migration seaward.
Parrot Bay	A name brand coconut flavored rum. Also comes in several other flavors.
parsley	See parsley under **Herbs**.
parsnip	The white, tapered, edible root of a plant from the parsley family that is used as a vegetable.
Passoa	A brand name passion fruit liqueur.
pasta	Italian. ❖ A dough made of flour, water and, sometimes, eggs. ❖ Processed store bought pasta that comes in many shapes and sizes, e.g., spaghetti, macaroni, and lasagna. ❖ A dish of cooked pasta.
pasteurization	The partial sterilization of liquid products such as milk, beer, wine, etc. so that they keep longer. ✓ Pasteurization is achieved by keeping the liquid at a high temperature (160 degrees F, 70 degrees C) long enough to destroy harmful bacteria without making any significant chemical changes to the liquid. This process was originally proposed by Louis Pasteur after whom it was named.
pastry	Sweet, baked goods made with shortened dough, i.e., pies and tarts.
pate	The French word for pastry. ❖ *Pate sucree*, a sweetened pastry. Used for *flans, tartlets,* and *pataisserie*. ❖ A ground or pounded, cooked and seasoned meat, game or fish mixture that is served cold, e.g., chicken liver *pate*. ❖ *Pate de foi gras* is a very rich pate and is made from goose liver and truffles. It is cooked in a terrine mold or in pastry.
patisserie	French. Pastry or small cake.

peach	A fruit from the rose family with a pinkish-yellow, fuzzy skin and sweet, juicy, orange-colored flesh containing one large seed (bone or stone).
peach brandy	A brandy flavored with fresh or dried peaches.
pear	A tear-shaped fruit of the rose family with a yellow to red skin and cream-colored, sweet flesh similar to that of an apple.
pearled barley	A small variety of barley that has had both the inner and outer husks removed and is then polished to a buff white color.
peas	A variety of legumes native to Europe. The long green pods contain round green seeds that are used as a vegetable. Depending on the variety, the whole pod may be eaten, such as snow peas.
pecan	A brown oblong hickory nut with a hard shell and a brown skinned two-part kernel with cream-colored flesh.
pectin	Substance in some fruits and vegetables that is used as a setting agent for preserves, jams and jellies.
peel	❖ The skin or rind of a vegetable or fruit. ❖ To remove the skin or rind.
Peking duck	Mandarin. A dish made with roasted duck meat and strips of crisp duck skin. The meat is topped with scallions and sauce, then wrapped in Mandarin pancakes.
penne	A small, tubular Italian pasta that is cut on the diagonal.
penuche	❖ Mexican. A fudge-like candy made with brown sugar, butter, cream or milk, and nuts. ❖ Spanish. An ear of corn or raw sugar.
pepper	See pepper under **Spices**.
pepperoni	A highly seasoned beef and pork Italian salami usually containing cayenne.
perch	A small freshwater fish native to European and American rivers and lakes.
persimmon	*Kaki.* The small, round, orange edible fruit of the persimmon tree.
pesto	An Italian sauce made of herbs, garlic, olive oil and grated cheese.
pese-sirop	French. Saccharometer. A sugar scale.
petite four	Small, dainty, glazed cakes such as genoise filled with chocolate, coffee, almond, praline, maraschino, Curaçao, or other butter cream.
pe-tsai	Chinese cabbage.

pheasant en plumage	A roasted male pheasant that is served in a life-like frame made of its own plumage.
phyllo	Greek. A very thin multi-layered pastry dough that is designed to produce a light, flaky pastry. Phyllo dough is easy to work with, quite versatile and is available in the freezer section of most grocery stores.
pickle	❖ The brine used in preserving or salting meats. ❖ Vegetables, such as onions and cucumbers that are soaked in brine then preserved in spiced vinegar.
pickling spice	A blend of herbs, spices and seeds used primarily in pickle making. Also used in marinades, shrimp, roast, and vegetables. For use in cooking, wrap securely in cheesecloth and tie with string.
pig's caul	*Crepin* (French). A membrane in the shape of a net covering the lower part of the pig's bowels.
pike	A freshwater food fish found in ponds, lakes, and rivers in northern Europe and America.
pilaf	A Turkish dish made of seasoned rice and sometimes meat.
pilsner	German. *Pilcsner*. A tall slender beer glass with a base. ❖ A light beer with a strong hops flavor.
pimiento	Pimento. A bright red variety of sweet peppers from which paprika is made and are used primarily for stuffing olives or as a garnish.
Pina Colada	❖ A tall bar drink made with light rum, coconut milk, and crushed pineapple blended with crushed ice. ❖ A party punch made with pineapple juice, coconut cream, coconut syrup or flavoring, cinnamon, pineapple soda, and vanilla ice cream. Add rum if desired.
pinch	Amount of an ingredient that is picked up between the thumb and finger.
pineapple	The large, oval-shaped fruit of the pineapple plant with a golden-brown outer skin that looks like a prickly tortoise shell containing sweet, succulent, yellow, fibrous flesh.
pineapple guava	*Feijoa*. The green edible fruit of a myrtle tree native to South America which are commercially grown in New Zealand.
pine nut	The edible seed of any of several pines, including the piñon but not limited to it. Pine-nuts grow inside the pine cone.
piñon	The dark brown, small, edible nut of a low-growing pine (piñon tree) native to the western U.S. Piñons grow inside a small pine cone.

pinot	A white, red or black variety of French grapes used in wine making.
pinot noir	❖ A black variety of French grapes. ❖ A dry red wine made from the same grape that Burgundy is made from.
pinto bean	See bean.
Pisang Ambon	An emerald green liqueur originally from Indonesia made from several tropical fruits and herbs native to the Emerald Belt (S. E. Asian Islands). ✓ It is no longer available in the U.S.
pisco	A Peruvian brandy.
piche-pache	A ragout made with turkey giblets.
pistachio	The nut of an Iranian tree, related to the cashew. The kernel is green and the shell is naturally beige, but is sometimes died red. ✓ Pistachios must be roasted for human consumption as they are toxic when raw.
pit	To remove stones, pits, or seeds from fruit.
pith	The white part of citrus fruit between the peel and the flesh.
pizza	Italian. Pizza pie. A flat, round of dough spread with a spicy tomato mixture and topped with cheese and other toppings, such as pepperoni, Canadian bacon, and/or mushrooms. Commonly associated with Italian cooking, though the name may stem from the German *pizzo*.
plantain	*Platano* (Spanish). A tropical fruit resembling a banana but larger and darker green with a thick peel. Usually served baked or fried.
platano	See plantain.
plat russe	❖ A Russian dish. ❖ A shallow, oval baking dish in various sizes for serving hot or cold food.
plum	The round, smooth-skinned fruit of a plum tree with a single oblong seed. The color and flavor of a plum depends on the variety.
poach	To cook gently in simmering but not boiling liquid. See Simmer. ✎ Poached eggs are cooked in butter over steaming water in an egg poacher. Crack the egg and drop into a cup containing one teaspoon butter. Cover with lid and cook to desired doneness.
polenta	An Italian cornmeal porridge.
pollack	A food fish native to the north Atlantic and Pacific oceans. Pollacks are from the cod family, but have a protruding jaw and are darker in color.

pomegranate	A large, red berry about the size of an orange with thick skin resembling a citrus rind. It is separated into several chambers and contains many seeds, each one encased in a succulent, tart aril.
pompano	A food fish native to the southern Atlantic and gulf coasts of North America.
poppy seed	See poppy seed under **Herbs**.
porcine	*Porcino*. A large, brown edible mushroom that is also sold in dried form.
porridge	Grain or legume meal mixed with milk or water and cooked until thick.
port	❖ A sweet fortified Portuguese wine with a rich taste and aroma. Named after the port city of Oporto because it was originally shipped from there. ❖ Wines that are similar to port but made in another region of the world.
portobello	Portabella or portabello. A mature cultivated button mushroom that is large, dark, fleshy, and rich in flavor.
posole	Mexican/southwestern U.S. A dish made with hominy and pork, and seasoned with red chili pods.
potato	Any of a variety of edible starchy tubers of the potato plant that are cultivated as a valuable food source.
pot roast	To cook a cut of meat or poultry, after browning in oil, by simmering or steaming slowly. ✎ Roasting may be done in the oven or on the stove top with a small amount of liquid or in its own juices. Use a covered casserole with a tight fitting lid. Root vegetables such as potatoes, carrots, and onions may be added for flavor and served on the side. ✓ Tougher cuts of meat become quite tender when cooked in this manner.
pound	To reduce to a powder or smooth paste. ✓ Use a heavy bowl and the end of a rolling pin if a mortar and pestle are not available.
pralin a conde	French. Egg white and powdered sugar whipped together and mixed with a large amount of chopped almonds. Used for pastries and sweets.
praline	French. ❖ Flavoring made of caramelized sugar and almonds. Used in sweet dishes. ❖ A confection of pecans or other nuts browned in boiling sugar. ❖ A piece of candy made of caramel and pecans.
prawn	An edible ten-legged crustacean that resembles shrimp.
preheat	To heat oven or broiler to desired temperature.

preserve	❖	Whole fruit preserved by boiling it with sugar and pectin to make jam or conserves.
	❖	To cure, smoke, can, or freeze foods for future use.
primeurs	❖	Early or forced fruit or vegetables.
	❖	The first fruits or vegetables of the season.

process cheese See cheese.

proscuitto Thin sliced, spicy Italian ham that has been dehydrated.

prune A dried plum.

prunelles A French liqueur made of fresh sloe plums.

puff pastry Feuilletage. A basic dough made of flour, butter, salt, and water.

Pumpernickel A dark grainy sourdough bread made with rye flour.

pumpkin A large round, orange variety of squash with a grooved surface and sweet, orange, firm flesh. The center is hollow with a viscous, fibrous network of seeds. Pumpkins are widely grown as a food source.
- ✓ Seeds may be roasted and eaten. Rinse seeds in warm water to remove fibers and gelatinous substance, spread out on a cookie sheet and sprinkle with salt. Roast in 350 degree F oven until golden brown.

pungent An enticing or stimulating aroma or flavor.

puree French. Fruit, vegetables or meat, usually precooked, that have been sieved or blended into a thick, smooth consistency, e.g., baby food.

Purple Haze A tall bar drink made with tequila, rum, vodka, gin, Royal Chambord, sour mix, and 7-Up over ice.

purslane *Verdolagas* (Spanish). A wild growing, trailing plant with succulent leaves and thick fleshy stalks that are used in salads and as a vegetable.

ptcha Jewish. Calf's foot jelly.

pytt i panna Swedish. Leftovers of roast beef, veal and ham mixed with chopped fried onions, diced boiled potatoes, sautéed in butter and served with a fried egg on top.

Notes:

Q

quarktorte	A German cottage cheese gateau.
quenelle	A poached dumpling made of finely ground fish and lettuce mixed with egg, butter, cream, and seasonings. Served with a cream sauce.
quesadilla	Mexican/southwestern U.S. A sandwich made of two flour tortillas filled with melted cheese and sometimes seasoning or chili. Usually served with sour cream, salsa, guacamole, and salsa.
quetsch	A pure white spirit originally distilled in the Alsace region of France from the fermented juice of plums.
quiche	Savory French custard, made with cheese, ham or fish and baked in a pastry shell.
quiche lorraine	A quiche made with cheese and bacon pieces.
quick bread	Any bread, biscuits, etc. made with baking powder or soda that can be baked quickly.
quince	An Asian apple-like fruit with yellow skin and firm flesh.

Notes:

R

raclette	A Swiss cheese dish made by melting the cheese and pouring it over toast or boiled potatoes.

radish	A variety of round, oval, or tapering roots of the mustard family that are red, pink, white, or black with a pungent peppery flavor. Used fresh, alone or in salads.
ragout	A spicy Italian stew made with meat, poultry, or game and vegetables in either brown or white sauce. Cooked slowly without thickening.
rahalou	A vegetable ragout.
rakott kaposza	Hungarian sauerkraut made with smoked bacon, pork, onions, garlic, and paprika. Topped with sour cream and baked.
ramen	Japanese. A mass of thin noodles that are cooked in a broth with small pieces of meat and vegetables.
ramekin	❖ A small individual size serving dish. ❖ A cheese dish made with eggs or bread crumbs in a mold or shell.
rare	❖ Underdone. ❖ Deep pink roasted or broiled meat. See *Saignant*.
rarebit	See Welsh rabbit.
rareripe	A fruit or vegetable that is forced to ripen prematurely.
raspberry	An edible red, yellow (gold), or black, many seeded fruit that grows on a thorny bramble. A raspberry is smaller than a blackberry and has a tart flavor.
raspberry brandy	A dry, white brandy distilled from raspberries. Originally made in Germany, Alsace, and Switzerland.
ravigote	A spiced vinegar sauce.
ravioli	An Italian pasta dish made of a savory meat sauce encased in small pockets of pasta.
Red Delicious	A deep red American grown apple with five peaks on the bottom end. Delicious apples are hardy and keep well through the winter.
Red Rum	A Virgin Island rum flavored with mango, pineapple, coconut, and berries.
reduce	*Reduire* (French). To boil down sauce or liquid to concentrate flavor and thicken the consistency.
refresh	To pour cold water over previously blanched and drained food. This process sets vegetable colors and cleans meats.
refrigerate	To store food at temperatures just above freezing (about 40 degrees F) so that the bacteria that cause foods to spoil are essentially hibernating.
relish	A condiment usually made with pickles, onions, and seasonings.

remouillage	French. Bones re-boiled in fresh water after the stock has been poured off once.
remoulade	A piquant French sauce.
render	French. To gently melt down fat into drippings in the oven and then strain or boil with a little water and strain again when clear.
rennet	A substance taken from the stomach membrane of animals which is used to separate fresh milk into curds and whey or to curdle sour milk. ✓ Rennet is used in making cheese. Rennet tablets may be used to make homemade cheeses and ice creams. These tablets are usually found in the gelatin and pudding section of the grocery store, but are difficult to find.
renverser	French. To turn food out of a mold or onto a dish.
restaurant	A place of business that serves food and drinks.
Rhine wine	❖ A wine such as Hock that is made from the grapes grown in the Rhine valley of west central Europe. ❖ A wine similar to a Rhine wine but made elsewhere. ✓ These white wines are known for their delicate bouquet.
rhubarb	An Asian plant with large dark green leaves and long, slender, red stalks. The leaves are poisonous but the stalks are used for food.
rice	The starchy seeds of a widely cultivated grain that are used as a food staple. Native to southeastern Asia.
ricotta	See cheese.
Riesling	A dry to very sweet white wine made from a single variety of grapes, originally grown in Germany.
risotto	Italian. A rice dish cooked in beef stock and seasoned with saffron or Parmesan.
rissoler	French. To bake or fry to a brown color in a hot oven. For example, *Pommes rissolées* are browned potatoes.
roast	❖ A cut of meat suitable for roasting. ❖ To cook using surrounding heat while well basted with fat. Roasting can be done in a Dutch oven over an open fire, on a stove top, or in an oven.
roaster	❖ A deep oval pan with a lid and handles that is used to make roasts or to cook large poultry such as turkeys. ❖ A food that is to be roasted and usually weighs over four pounds, e.g., poultry or a cut of beef, pork, or game.
roesti	Swiss. Grated vegetables or thinly sliced fruits that have been sautéed in butter. ✎ Potato roesti is grated potatoes formed into cakes and sautéed in butter.

- Apple roesti is a dish of thinly sliced apples sautéed in butter with onions, cinnamon, and cloves. Then baked with bread slices, beaten eggs, and sugar until golden.

romaine	Cos lettuce. A garden lettuce with long, crisp, dark green leaves and a long head.
Romano	See cheese.
Roquefort	See cheese.
rosé	A light pink originally French table wine made from red grapes.
	✓ The skins are removed after fermentation has begun in order to retain a just a touch of crimson.
rosemary	See rosemary under **Herbs**.
Rose's Sweetened Lime Juice	A sweetened lime juice created by Lauchlin Rose in 1876, Edinburgh, Scotland. Made by a patented method of preserving lime juice without alcohol.
rostbraten	Austrian. Sirloin steak cut from the fat end, flattened, and pan fried or stewed.
roti	❖ Hindi. A round, flat, unleavened bread.
	❖ A sandwich made with roti wrapped around a filling.
rotisserie	An appliance or barbecue rack with a spit that rotates over an open flame. Usually used to cook meat.
roughy	A popular food fish, i.e., orange roughy.
rouille	French. A peppery garlic sauce.
roulade	French. A slice of stuffed meat that is rolled, browned, and steamed or braised.
roux	French. A fat and flour mixture that is the basis of all flour sauces whether white, yellow, or brown.
	- The amount of fat added is generally about the same as that of flour. Melt fat, remove from heat, stir in flour and pour into water, stock, or milk. Stir over heat until thickened. Season, bring to a boil and cook.

Roux blanc   White sauce. Two cups flour cooked slowly in 1 2 cups clarified butter while stirring continuously and kept white. Used for white sauces and soups.

Roux blonde   Yellow sauce. Two cups flour cooked in 1 2 cups of clarified butter to a light yellow color.

Roux brun   Brown sauce. Two cups flour browned very slowly in 1 2 cups of clarified butter or clarified drippings.

Royal Chambord	A trade mark high quality French raspberry liqueur.
rubaboo	A type of soup.
rum	An alcoholic beverage dating back to the 1700's, originating in the Caribbean Islands and made from distilling fermented cane juice or molasses. The flavor and aroma depend on the distillation process and the color relies on how it is aged. Rum aged in oak is gold or brown. Clear rum is made by aging it in steel. ✓ Puerto Rican rum, which is traditionally white or silver, is clear with a light flavor and body. Gold and amber rums are deeper in color and flavor. Cuban and Jamaican rums are rich and full-bodied. Some rums are flavored with herbs, spices, or fruit.
rumaki	An Asian appetizer made with chicken livers and water chestnuts in a marinade of soy sauce, peanut oil, sake, sugar, ginger, and lemon zest. The mixture is wrapped in a slice of bacon and broiled until the bacon is crisp.
rummer	A large elaborate, footed drinking glass of German or Dutch origin.
Rum Runner	A tall bar drink made with orange, pineapple and cranberry juice, Malibu, and blackberry brandy on ice.
rutabaga	A thick edible yellow root from the turnip family.
rye	A widely cultivated grass whose grain is ground and used as a flour.

Notes:

_____
_____
_____
_____
_____
_____
_____
_____
_____
_____

sabayon	Italian. *Zabaglione*. An Italian topping made by whipping egg yolks, sugar, and Marsala wine together. Served over fruit.
sacher torte	An Austrian chocolate gateau.
saddle	A cut of meat in which both sides of the unsplit back of an animal including both loins are still joined together.

saffron	See saffron under **Herbs**.
sage	See sage under **Herbs**.
saignant	Extremely rare. The blood runs out when the meat is cut. Usually referring to roasted or broiled meat or game.
saithe	See pollack.
saimin	A Hawaiian noodle soup.
sake	Japanese. *Saki*. An alcoholic beverage made by fermenting rice. Usually served hot.
salami	Italian. A fresh or dried pork or beef sausage that is cured, salted, and spiced.
salep	A starchy edible meal ground from the roots of certain orchids.
salmis	Italian. A form of ragout, usually made of game or poultry which is lightly roasted then cut up and gently simmered for a short time in a rich, brown sauce.
salmon	A large migratory fish that lives in both salt and fresh water. Native to the cold coastal waters and rivers of North America and Europe. Salmon has flesh that ranges from red-orange to peach in color.
saloop	British. Sassafras tea. An infusion of aromatic herbs used as a hot beverage.
salpicon	❖ Meat, poultry, or fish cut into very small cubes for small ragouts. ❖ Finely diced fruit for dessert dishes.
salsa	Spanish. A spicy sometimes hot sauce made with tomatoes, onions, and hot peppers.
salsify	A long carrot-like root native to Europe with yellowish-white or black skin and a pleasant flavor. Used as a vegetable.
salt	Sodium chloride crystals used to season or preserve food. The following are some common types of salt:

	table salt	A white, fine textured, sodium chloride crystal that is used to season or preserve food. Iodized or non-iodized.
	sea salt	Fine textured salt crystals derived from dehydrated sea water.
	kosher salt	Coarse textured salt crystals approved for use by Jewish law.
	rock salt	A large or granular crystal of unrefined salt (halite) that is used mostly for making homemade ice cream and for de-icing walkways.

salt-cured	Meat that has been preserved with salt or brine.
salt-rising bread	A pungent bread dating back to the eighteen hundreds that uses salt as a leavening agent and is made of milk, flour, corn meal, sugar, and salt.

Salty Dog	A tall bar drink made with grapefruit juice, gin or vodka, and salt over ice.
salver	A tray or serving platter.
samlet	See parr.
sangaree	Spanish. A sweet iced drink made with wine, ale, beer or other liquor and garnished with nutmeg.
sangria	Spanish. A punch made with orange juice, red wine, sugar, brandy, and Cointreau. Club soda is added when serving. Garnished with citrus slices.
sardine	A small marine food fish that resembles herring and is native to the Atlantic coasts and the Mediterranean.
sarmale	Romanian. Sauerkraut rolls made with ground beef and pork, boiled rice, and seasoned with garlic, salt, pepper, and chopped onions. Wrapped in leaves of pickled cabbage. Braised and served with sour cream.
sarsaparilla	Spanish. ❖ The roots of the tropical sarsaparilla plant that are used as flavoring. ❖ A sweet carbonated drink that is flavored with sassafras and birch oil extract.
sassafras	Spanish. ❖ The North American tree from which the roots are taken and used as flavoring. ✓ Classed as a carcinogen and no longer used as flavoring.
sauce pan	A small or medium sized deep pan with a handle.
sauerbraten	German. Beef that has been marinated in a mixture of vinegar, onions, garlic, pepper, and bay leaves, then roasted.
sauerkraut	Thinly cut cabbage that is salted and fermented in its own brine.
sausage	❖ A highly seasoned minced meat stuffed in casings of prepared animal intestine or man-made casing. ❖ A link or patty of finely chopped highly seasoned meat. Usually pork.
sauté	French. To brown food in butter or in an oil and butter mixture.
sauter	French. A quick cooking process in which the food is browned rapidly in a *sauté* pan by tossing food in hot fat over high heat.
Sauterne	❖ A full-bodied sweet, white French wine from the Sauternes district. There are three varieties of Sauterne: dry, sweet, and Haute Sauterne. ❖ In the U.S., Sauterne refers to any wine, dry or sweet, that is made from a blend of grapes.

Sauterne punch	A party punch made with cold champagne, cold Chablis, cognac, and Curaçao. Served over ice.
Sauvignon blanc	A dry white French wine made from grapes originally grown in the Bordeaux region and the Loire Valley.
savarin	A rich French yeast cake baked in a ring mold, then soaked in rum or kirsch syrup.
saveloy	Italian. A highly seasoned, dry sausage made of salted pork.
savory	❖ Sour or salty. ❖ A dish without sugar. ❖ A small, piquant dish, traditionally served in Britain as the last course to cleanse the palate after dessert in preparation for a glass of port, i.e., Welsh rarebit or other snacks that are served on toast or crackers. ❖ An aromatic herb. See savory under **Herbs**.
Savoy	French. A cabbage with wrinkled, curly leaves and a compact head. Named for the Savoy region of France.
scald	❖ To plunge into boiling water for easier peeling. ❖ To heat a liquid to just below the boiling point.
scallop	❖ A marine mollusk that has an almost circular shell with ribs that radiate out from the center and a scalloped edge. European scallops are larger than those found in the U.S. ❖ The succulent adductor muscle of a sea scallop which is used as food. ❖ A dish or pan, usually the shell of a scallop, in which oysters and seafood dishes are cooked and/or served. ❖ To bake food in a casserole with liquid or sauce, often topped with bread crumbs.
scallopini	Italian. See escalope.
scampi	Italian. *Caramote*. A large shrimp that is prepared in a garlic sauce.
schnapps	❖ Shnahps. German. Brandy. ❖ Schnaps. A strong Holland gin.
schnitzel	German. A breaded and seasoned veal cutlet that has been sautéed in butter. Usually served with noodles and garnished with lemon slices.
schwarzwälder kirschtorte	German. A chocolate, cherry-flavored cake filled with whipped cream and cherries.
scone	Scottish. ❖ A thin oatmeal cake, baked on a griddle, such as a teacake or soda biscuit. ❖ A rich quick bread cut into triangular shapes and cooked on a griddle or baked.

Scooby Snack	A short bar drink made with Malibu or Parrot Bay, Madori, pineapple juice, and half-and-half.
score	To mark with a series of shallow, even cuts.
Scotch	Scotch Whisky. A smoky flavored whisky originally made in Scotland from 100% malted barley. Distilled five to fifteen years in old-fashioned pot stills. There are three types of Scotch whisky:

> **malt whisky** — Made from 100% malted barley and distilled in old-fashioned pot stills.
> **grain whisky** — Made from unmalted wheat and corn mixed with malted barley. It is distilled in large industrial continuous stills. These whiskies have a natural flavor and taste and are primarily used in blends.
> **blended whisky** — Made by combining almost fifty different grain and malt whiskies. Approximately 95% of all Scotch whiskies are sold are blended.

Screwdriver	A bar drink made from orange juice and vodka on ice.
scup	A marine food fish native to the Atlantic U. S.
seafood	All varieties of marine food fish.
sea kale	A Eurasian herb from the mustard family. Its roots and leaf-stalks are used as vegetables.
sea lettuce	Ulva. A seaweed that is used as a lettuce.
sear	To seal in the natural juices, usually of meat, by frying over intense heat for a short time. Often done before made into a stew or casserole.
sea salt	See salt.
seasoning	Seasonings include salt, pepper, herbs, spices, and other flavorings. ✓ To "correct seasoning" is to taste the preparation before it is completely cooked and make any necessary adjustments.
seedcake	A sweet cake or cookie containing aromatic seeds such as caraway or poppy.
seeds	The aromatic grains of certain plants that are used for food and can germinate to create more plants.
seidel	Greek. A large beer glass.
semolina	The purified gritty or grain-like remains of wheat after it has gone a bolting machine. Semolina is used in making pasta.
sesame seed	See sesame seed under **Herbs**.

seviche	A Mexican appetizer made of raw fish such as grouper, shrimp, or squid that is marinated in a mixture of fresh lime juice, onions, tomatoes, garlic, salt, and sometimes seasoned with jalapeños.
sewt yee	Chinese. Snow fungus. A white, edible mushroom that grows on the sides of trees.
Sex on the Beach	A tall bar drink made with cranberry juice, grapefruit juice, one ounce vodka, and 3/4 ounce peach schnapps. Stir and serve over ice. ✎ To make a Sex on the Beach punch: Mix together one cup each of strawberry schnapps, rum, Medori, and raspberry liqueur. Add 1 1/2 quarts each of pineapple juice and cranberry juice. Stir in one bag of ice.
shad	A North Atlantic, wide bodied, food fish from the herring family. Shad roe is harvested for use as caviar.
sha cha sauce	A Chinese spicy sauce used as a dipping sauce or as a marinade.
shaddock	A pear-shaped citrus fruit.
shallot	A bulbous perennial herb with small clustered bulbs, similar to garlic. Shallots have a milder flavor than garlic and are used for seasoning dishes and in pickling. ✓ Substituting shallots for garlic in some dishes can make a subtle, tasty difference in the aroma and flavor.
Shamrock	A tall bar drink made with Irish whiskey, dry vermouth, and a dash of crème de menthe. Served over ice and garnished with an olive.
Sharkbite	A short bar drink made with Captain Morgan, light rum, Blue Curaçao, sour mix, and a splash of grenadine as garnish.
Shepherd's bread	A yeast bread made of flour, milk, sugar, butter, and yeast. The dough is shaped into a large ball and baked.
Shepherd's pie	A meat pie baked in a crust made of mashed potatoes.
sherbet	Sherbert. *Sorbet* (French). An originally Persian frozen mixture similar to ice cream and made of milk, egg whites, gelatin, and fruit juice.
sherry	❖ A fortified wine with a nutty flavor. Originally of Jerez, Spain. ❖ Wines similar to the original sherry but produced in other areas of the world.
shiitake	Japanese. A dark, Asian mushroom with a savory flavor.
shoat	A young hog.
shortbread	A round cake make with shortening, butter, and flavored with vanilla or lemon zest.

shortening	Fat which, when worked into flour, gives a crisp (short) quality to pastry and cakes. This includes both lard and vegetable shortening. ✓ Fats with the least liquid have the greatest shortening power.
short pastry	*Pate a foncer fine* (French). A basic dough made of flour, sugar, butter, egg, salt, and water.
shot	See jigger.
shoyu	Japanese. Soy sauce.
shred	To cut or break into uneven strips.
shrimp	A small shellfish related to the lobster. The most common variety is the gray shrimp which turns pink when cooked. The following are those most widely available:

Salad shrimp	Tiny pink, peeled, pre-cooked shrimp commonly used in salads. They are sold by the pound.
Medium shell-on shrimp	Vary from 52 to 60 count per pound.
Large shell-on shrimp	Range between 43 and 50 count per pound.
Jumbo shell-on shrimp	Fluctuate between 36 and 42 count per pound.
Colossal shell-on shrimp	Under 10 count per pound.

✓ Shrimp are sold in a variety of ways: skin-on, peeled, and peeled and pre-cooked. It is best to order or buy shrimp by the count per pound.

sieve	❖ Colander. A perforated bowl or utensil used for straining foods. ❖ To work through a sieve or food mill to obtain a fine substance or puree.
sift	To shake a dry, powdered substance through a sieve or sifter to remove any lumps and lend lightness to it. Usually refers to flour or sugar.
simmer	To cook in liquid at 195 degrees F (90 degrees C) or just below the boiling point so that bubbles occasionally break the surface.
simnel	❖ A British fruit cake that is coated with almond paste. Usually made for mid lent Sunday, Easter, and Christmas. ❖ A crisp bread or bun made of fine wheat flour.
Singapore sling	A tall bar drink made with sour mix, gin, grenadine, cherry brandy, and carbonated water. Served over ice and garnished with a maraschino cherry.
sippet	British. A small piece of toast or fried bread soaked in gravy or used as a garnish.
skewer	A long pointed metal or wooden utensil used to hold small pieces of food together such as meats, vegetables and/or fruits for roasting over an open fire or on a grill. A skewer is used to make kabobs.

skillet	❖ Frying pan. ❖ A pan with feet used for cooking over an open fire.
skim	To remove impurities such as fat or scum from the surface of sauces, soups or stocks after the liquid as been slowly brought to a boil.
sling	A bar drink made with a base of liquor, sugar or sweet liqueur, and lemon juice. Mixed with water if served hot and carbonated water if served over ice.
slivovitz	*Slivowitz*. A European white, dry plum brandy distilled with the crushed plum seeds. Originally made in Yugoslavia, Hungary, and Romania.
sloe	❖ A variety of plum. ❖ The white brandy made from sloe plums.
sloe gin	A sweet reddish liqueur with a gin base that is flavored with sloe plums.
Sloe Screw	A bar drink made with sloe gin and orange juice.
smearcase	See cheese.
smeddum	Ground malt powder.
smelt	A small silvery food fish that lives in both salt and fresh water. Native to the Atlantic and Pacific coasts.
snails	*Escargot* (French). The only edible mollusk that can live both on land and in the water. 🥄 To prepare, wash and remove top, blanch in water with a small amount of vinegar, and drain. Remove snails from shells. Cut and dispose of black vein. Braise snails in a stock made with white wine and herbs. Let cool and serve in their shells.
snail butter	*Beurre pour les escargots* (French). Creamed butter mixed with finely chopped shallots and garlic, chopped parsley, salt, and pepper. Served with snails.
snapper	A widely eaten warm water marine food fish.
snifter	❖ A short-stemmed, pear-shaped liquor glass with a narrow opening used for serving brandy. ❖ A small drink of distilled liquor.
Sno-cone	A tall, icy bar drink made with layers of grenadine, raspberry or blueberry schnapps, and Blue Curaçao poured over shaved ice and filled with 7-Up.
snow peas	See peas.
sole	A flat, marine food fish native to the western European coastline and the Baltic Sea.

Sorbet	French. *Sorbetto* or *granita* (Italian). An originally Persian frozen mixture made with fruit juice. See sherbet.
sorghum	❖ *Sorgo*. A cereal grain similar to corn. ❖ The syrup from the juice of sorgo that resembles cane syrup.
sorpaparo	A Creole dish of onions sautéed in butter with Worcestershire, pepper, and mustard. Usually served with beef.
sorrel	Wood sorrel. A garden herb used as a vegetable or for flavoring soups and sauces.
soubise	A sauce made with onions, butter, flour, milk, and white pepper.
soufflé	A French dish made with beaten egg whites. A soufflé is similar to a mousse but lighter in consistency. It can be hot or cold, sweet or savory. ✓ A soufflé should rise 1 to 2 inches above the rim of the soufflé dish.
soufflé dish	A round, oven-proof, deep dish with straight sides. Used for making souffles in.
soup	A liquid food with a meat, fish, or vegetable stock and sometimes containing small pieces of food. ✓ *Soup du Jour* (French). Soup of the day.
sour	A bar drink made with liquor, lemon or lime juice, sugar, and ice.
sour cream	Real sour cream is cream that has turned sour through the action of natural bacteria. Cultured sour cream is made with cultured milk and cream, along with other ingredients and additives.
sour dough	Dough made with a fermented dough starter which is used as leavening.
sour mix	A non-alcoholic bar mixture similar to a concentrated lemonade. Used as a base in mixed drinks.
souse	To cover food in wine vinegar and/or wine, and spices. Cook slowly and allow food to cool in the same liquid.
Southern Comfort	A brand name peach-flavored bourbon liqueur. Produced in St. Louis, Missouri. It is available in 100 proof (50% alcohol) and 76 proof (38% alcohol).
South Hampton	A tall bar drink made with tonic water, a squeeze of lime juice, and Angostura. Served over ice and garnished with a lime slice.
soy sauce	Chinese. A brown liquid sauce made through the process of fermenting soy beans for a long period of time, then soaking them in a brine solution.
spatchcock	❖ A term used in broiling. ❖ Any very small bird split down the back, flattened out and basted well with melted butter.

The Ultimate Kitchen Consultant

spatula	❖ A long-handled metal kitchen tool with a flattened end, used for lifting and flipping foods, such as eggs.
	❖ A kitchen tool with a flat rubber or silicone end, used to mix batters and other soft mixes. Aids in lifting and folding.
spaetzle	German. Swiss. *Spaetzli*. Small dumplings made with flour, eggs, nutmeg, and pepper. Made by pressing the dough through a sieve into boiling water, then baked until golden brown.
spaghetti	Italian. A pasta that is long and thin, resembling string.
spearmint	See spearmint under **Herbs**.
spices	The aromatic products such as the dried fruit, buds, flowers, seeds, leaves, bark, or roots of certain plants.
spinach	A dark green leafy herb that is used as a vegetable.
spirits	The distilled ethyl alcohol and water that is derived from an alcoholic liquid, i.e., hard liquor.
sponge cake	A light cake that is made without shortening or other fat, such as angel food cake.
spoon bread	A soft bread that is served with a spoon. Made with cornmeal, milk, eggs, and butter or shortening.
sprat	A small herring-like food fish, similar to an anchovy, found on the Atlantic coast of England.
springform pan	A round cake pan with sides that clamp together, forming a leak proof seal around the bottom of the pan.
squab	A very young pigeon.
squash	Any of a variety of edible gourds that come in various sizes, shapes and colors, and are cultivated for food.
squid	An edible ten-armed cephalopod similar to an octopus.
	✓ The upper side must be opened and the ink sac removed before preparation.
Squirrel	A short bar drink made with vodka, orange juice, and sweetened lime juice.
stachy	Chinese artichoke. The tender artichoke flavored roots of a plant that are used as a vegetable.
star anise	Chinese. A small, firm, star-shaped seed with a licorice flavor that is used to flavor meat and poultry, especially in stew. It is one of the ingredients in five-spice powder.
star fruit	See carambola.

starter	A fermented mixture or substance, containing microorganisms, that is used to create fermentation in another mixture.
steak tartare	French. A meat dish made by combining ground round steak with capers, anchovies, onions, Worcestershire, red wine, brandy, and mustard. The beef mixture is formed into a patty and a well is made in the center of it. A beaten egg yolk is placed in the well just before serving. Steak tartare is served raw.
steam	❖ To cook food in a steamer over a pan of boiling water until the food is tender. ✓ Food may be steamed in a microwave oven. Pour a small amount of water into a glass bowl. Place the food in the bowl and cover. Cook on high for periods of two minutes at a time. Remove when the food is tender but not fully cooked.
steep	To soak in a hot but not boiling liquid.
steinhäger	German. A rectified white, grain brandy flavored with juniper berries and other flavorings.
steirisches schoepsernes	Austrian. Stewed mutton made with root vegetables, sliced onions, and potatoes.
stekt fläsk	Swedish. Bacon cooked with pinto beans until thick and served sliced.
stew	To simmer meat, vegetables, fish, or poultry in liquid in a covered pan for a few hours. Suited to coarse-fibered or tough meats.
Stinger	A tall bar drink made with white créme de menthe and brandy over ice.
stir	To mix with a spoon, spatula, or fork in a circular motion.
stir-fry	To stir food briskly while it is frying.
stock	A clear soup made by simmering meat, bones, or vegetables in water or other liquid for several hours. Used for making gravy, sauce, and soup. ✎ Fish stock is made by simmering fish bones with root vegetables, herbs and seasonings in water for 20 minutes.
stöllen	German. A sweet yeast bread with fruit and nuts.
stout	A very dark, malt ale.
stroganoff	Russian. A sauce made with onions, garlic, butter, flour, beef stock, sour cream, mushrooms, Worcestershire, and sometimes beef. Usually served over noodles.
stuffing	See dressing.
sturgeon	A marine or freshwater food fish found on the Pacific coast and in almost all seas. A source of caviar.

succotash	A seasoned buttered or creamed dish made with cooked sweet corn and Lima beans.
suckling	A young animal, usually a pig or sheep, that has not been weaned.
suet	Finely ground beef fat without a membrane, preferably taken from around the kidney.
sugar	Sucrose crystals that are used as a sweetener or preservative. The following are some types of sugar:

    Granulated sugar   White, brittle, fine textured sucrose crystals that are obtained from sugarcane or sugar beets through a refining process. It is very sweet and has no flavor.

    Brown sugar   Dark brown or golden brown crystals that are covered with a dark syrup. It is less refined and has less sweetening power than granulated sugar and a light molasses flavor.

    Raw sugar   Beige, brittle, unrefined crystals that are less sweet than brown sugar with a hint of molasses flavor.

    Powdered or confectioner's sugar   A finely ground refined sugar.

sui rice	An Asian rice dish made of onions sautéed in oil with garlic, soy sauce, and rice. Simmered in clarified meat stock.
summer sausage	Any smoked or dried sausage that keeps without being refrigerated.
summer squash	Any squash that is picked before it is ripe.
sundae	Originally named *Sunday* for the day on which it was traditionally eaten. A dessert dish made with ice cream that is topped with fruit and/or syrup, nuts, and whipped cream. Sometimes garnished with a maraschino cherry.
Susu sauce	Susu. A creamed curry made with coconut milk.
svenks panna	Swedish. Veal and pork with slices of calf's kidney, seasoned, and sautéed in butter. Placed in stock with potatoes and stewed in the oven.
sweat	To draw out flavor by cooking diced or sliced vegetables gently in a little melted butter until soft, not browned, in a covered pan.
Swedish punch	Caloric punch. A highly alcoholic compound with a rum or arrack base. Flavored with spices and other flavorings. Served neat or mixed with hot water.
sweet and sour	See sour mix.
sweet breads	The pancreas or thymus of a calf used as food.

Sweet Dreams	A hot toddy made with hot chocolate and Malibu. Topped with whipped cream, cinnamon or nutmeg, and chocolate shavings.
sweet potato	A large, sweet tuber, unrelated to the potato, that is usually baked and eaten as a vegetable.
Swiss chard	See chard.
swordfish	A large marine fish found in the Atlantic, Pacific, and the Mediterranean. Swordfish is a popular game and food fish, and can weigh up to 400 pounds.
syrup	❖ Sugar and water boiled together to a specified temperature or consistency. Used in poaching and candying fruit, and in fresh fruit salad, etc. ❖ A store bought or homemade corn syrup that is made from sugar, water, and cornstarch. ❖ A store bought maple flavored syrup used to pour over pancakes or waffles. ❖ Liquid obtained from other sources of sugar, e.g., real maple syrup. ✎ Stock syrup: 1 cup granulated sugar dissolved in 2 cups water over gentle heat. Bring to a boil and boil for 10 minutes. Used for mixing with icing to give it a glossy appearance.
szechwan	A Chinese style of cooking that is hot and spicy, typically made with oils, hot spices, and sake.

Notes:

_____
_____
_____
_____
_____
_____
_____
_____
_____
_____

T

Tabasco	The trademark for a Texan hot sauce made from the Tabasco chili.
taco	Mexican/southwestern U.S. ✎ Hard taco. A fried corn tortilla or pre-made taco shell filled with meat that has been seasoned with chili and onions, topped with shredded lettuce, diced tomatoes, and grated cheese then folded in half. ✎ Soft taco. Prepared in the same way as a hard taco but in a soft flour tortilla.
tafia	A West Indian spirit distilled from molasses.

tagliatelli	Italian. *Tagliatelle*. See fettuccini.
tahini	Arabic. Sesame paste. A smooth paste made from sesame seeds.
tailli kataif	A Turkish dish made with noodles that have been cooked in milk then covered in a raisin syrup.
tamale	A Mexican/Southwestern U.S. dish in which meat and chili are rolled into a cornmeal dough which is then wrapped in corn husks and steamed.
tamis	French. Tammy. A sieve made of hair or a very fine meshed sieve for straining food.
tandoor	Hindi. A cylinder shaped clay oven in which food is cooked over hot coals or charcoal.
tang	❖ A pungent flavor, taste, or odor. ❖ Tang spelled with a capital *t* is a brand name sweetened, orange-flavored drink mix.
tangelo	A citrus fruit that is a hybrid cross between a mandarin orange and a grapefruit.
tangerine	Any of several mandarin oranges that have a deep orange peel and pulp.
tankard	A tall drinking vessel with one handle most often made of silver or pewter, and generally has a lid.
tapioca	A nutritious starchy substance obtained from the roots of the tropical cassava plant that is used in puddings and as a thickener. Tapioca is marketed in flaked, pearl, granulated, and flour form.
tarhonya	Small Hungarian noodles made of flour and eggs that are fried then cooked in bouillon and served with goulash.
tarragon	See tarragon under **Herbs**.
tart	❖ An open fruit, custard or jelly pie, e.g., fresh strawberry pie. ❖ A pastry pocket filled with pudding or pie filling. ✓ Line pastry shell with wax paper and weigh down with beans to keep pastry from bubbling. Bake until golden brown. Remove paper weight and fill as desired.
tartar sauce	A sauce made of mayonnaise and pickles. Usually served with fish.
tartlet	French. Tartelette. Small tarts served as appetizers.
tea	❖ The leaves and buds of a shrub, native to China and from the Theaceae family, that are grown and sorted into types (green, black, or oolong) and size (orange pekoe pekoe or souchong). ❖ A beverage made by steeping tea leaves or herbs in water.

	❖ An afternoon snack, i.e., cookies or sandwiches, served with tea.
teff	An African cereal grass that is ground into a white flour.
teiglach	A confection made by boiling a ball of dough in honey.
tempeh	An Asian dish prepared by fermenting soybeans with mold fungus.
tempura	Japanese. Seafood, usually shrimp, or vegetables dipped in an egg and flour batter
tenderize	To break down tough meat fibers and make them more tender by heating, marinating, or beating with a mallet.
tender loin	The large internal loin muscle located on each side of the spine which is the most tender cut of meat.
tequila	A Mexican liquor distilled from the sap from the agave plant mixed with the fermented agave juice (pulque) that is fermented for about two and a half days. The mix is then double distilled producing a pure white tequila. Gold tequila is aged in oak casks for up to four years. Mezcal is produced by a similar process, but does not come from the same region of Mexico.
Tequila Sunrise	A tall bar drink made with orange juice, tequila, and grenadine floated to the bottom of the glass. Garnished with an orange slice and a maraschino cherry.
teriyaki	Japanese. A sauce made with soy sauce, sake, sugar, ginger, garlic, and lemon zest. Used as a marinade or sauce for meat, chicken, or fish.
terrapin	A small aquatic turtle found along the south Atlantic coast of the U.S. and in the Ottawa river area that is used for food.
terrine	❖ A seasoned meat mixture similar to that used for a pate but usually has a coarser texture. ❖ An oval china or pottery mold in which the terrine is cooked.
tetrazinni	An Italian pasta and poultry dish cooked in a white sauce of chicken stock, vermouth or sherry, cream, mushrooms, grated Parmesan, and nutmeg.
Texas Tea	A party punch made with tequila, rum, vodka, gin, bourbon, triple sec, and sour mix stirred together. Pour in some Coke and serve over ice.
thyme	See thyme under **Herbs**.
tilapia	A popular African freshwater food fish from the cichlid family with a delicate aroma and flavor.
timbale	French. ❖ A half-conical mold in various sizes. ❖ A type of hot meat loaf.

	❖ A half-conical silver dish with a flat bottom for serving fine dishes and vegetables.
tiramisu	An Italian dessert made with ladyfingers, mascarpone, chocolate, and espresso.
toddy	❖ A hot alcoholic beverage made with hot water, liquor or brandy, brown sugar, lemon juice, and spices such as cinnamon, cloves, ginger, and/or nutmeg. Sometimes flavored with apple juice rather than lemon juice. ❖ A long bar drink similar to a sling but made with plain water.
toffee	Toffy. Taffy. A chewy candy made from boiling sugar and butter together which is then pulled into long ropes until it cools and holds its shape.
tofu	❖ Soy bean curd. ❖ A soft Japanese cheese made from soybean milk.
Tokay	❖ A white or plum colored grape from Tokay, Hungary. ❖ A sweet wine made from the Tokay grape, produced in the area of Tokay. ❖ A California wine which is a blend of Angelica, port, and sherry.
tomatillos	The small, round, tomato-like, edible fruit of a Mexican cherry plant which is similar to the tomato plant, with green, yellow or purplish skin. Used as a vegetable.
tomato	The fruit of the widely cultivated tomato plant which comes in a variety of shapes and sizes, and ranges from yellow to red in color. The tomato is smooth skinned with a pulpy, juicy center that contains many seeds. Used fresh as vegetables and in salads, or stewed.
tomato paste	A thick paste made entirely of tomatoes.
tomato sauce	A sauce made of tomato paste, onions, garlic, bell pepper, salt, and water.
Tom Collins	A tall bar drink made with gin, sour mix, 7-Up, and garnished with a lime slice.
tonic water	A carbonated beverage containing quinine and flavored with lemon and lime.
topinambour	See Jerusalem artichoke.
torte	A German cake made with several eggs, flour, sugar, finely ground nuts, and lemon zest. Covered with butter cream frosting and sprinkled with walnuts.
Tornado	A tall bar drink made with whisky, rum, tequila, vodka, Coke, and sugar. Served over ice.
tortilla	Mexican/southwestern U.S. ❖ A flour dough that is rolled out into a round shape. Leavened with baking powder or baking soda and cooked on a griddle. ❖ An unleavened, corn meal dough that is rolled out into a round shape and cooked on a griddle.

tortilla soup	Mexican. A spicy soup made of corn tortillas torn into strips or small portions, which are cooked in a base of beef stock, red chili peppers, tomatoes, onions, garlic and cilantro. Garnished with shredded cheddar cheese.
toss	To evenly distribute ingredients by turning them over and over again, either by hand or with two spoons.
tournedos	The tip of a filet mignon wrapped in a slice of bacon and sautéed.
tourtierre	French. Pork pie.
treacle	Molasses. Golden syrup. A table syrup made from a combination of molasses, sugar and corn syrup.
trencher	French. A wooden platter for serving food.
trigo	Spanish. Wheat.
tripe	A part of an animal stomach. The paunch of an animal stomach is plain tripe and the reticulum is honeycomb tripe.
triple sec	A generic brand, strong, clear orange liqueur. Triple sec literally means it is triple dry and triple distilled.
triticum	A type of wheat.
Tropical Sunrise	A tall bar drink made with crushed ice, Captain Morgan, triple sec, orange juice, pineapple juice, and grenadine. Garnished with a maraschino cherry.
Tropical Waters	A tall bar drink made with Blue Curaçao, Midori, and Sprite on ice.
trout	A species of salmon that is found in cold, clear water throughout the world and used as a food fish.
truffle	*Truffe* (French). ❖ A large, rare, dark edible mushroom that grows beneath the ground's surface. Considered a delicacy. ❖ Candy made from chocolate, sugar, and butter which is then rolled into small balls and coated with cocoa. Truffles sometimes contain liquor.
truss	To bind the legs and wings securely to the body of a fowl, i.e., turkey, chicken, and so forth.
tscheburek	Russian. Squares of noodle dough that are rolled out and filled with ground mutton, boiled rice, chopped bacon, diced tomatoes, chopped dill, parsley and seasoning. Pinched closed and sautéed in butter.
tumbler	A drinking glass without a stem.

tuna	❖ An albacore or bluefish that is used as a food fish. Sold as steaks and canned. ❖ Spanish. An edible prickly pear from a tuna (cactus) that can be made into jelly.
turbot	A large marine food fish resembling halibut but fuller, rounder and more delicate in flavor.
tureen	Turrine (French). A large, deep bowl used to serve soup from.
turlu	Turkish. A stew made of diced mutton, chopped onions, tomatoes, pumpkin, red peppers, eggplants, and green beans sweated in butter and seasoned. Moistened with very little water.
turnip	An herb from the mustard family with long, bulb shaped edible roots and green tops that are used as vegetables.
turnspit	A rotating spit (a slim metal rod used to roast meat over an open fire).
turtle	A marine reptile used as a food fish. The best green turtles come from the West Indies, Cuba, and Florida. Used mainly for soup.
Twister	A tall bar drink made with lemon-lime soda, vodka, and fresh lime juice.
tyee	A food fish.
tzimmes	Jewish. A sweet vegetable, fruit stew, or casserole. Served as an entree or to complement meat and fish.

Notes:

U V

ulva	Sea lettuce. An edible seaweed.
veal	A newborn calf used for food.
veloute	One of the basic French sauces made with butter, flour, and chicken stock.
verjus	French. Verjuice. The juice of unripe fruit especially sour grapes or crab apples.

vermouth	A dry or sweet French aperitif or liqueur flavored with aromatic herbs and usually used in mixed drinks.
vesiga	A jelly-like substance found around the spinal marrow of the sturgeon. *Visiga* is marketed dry and swells to five times its volume when it is soaked. It is used to make *culibijaka* and other Russian patties.
vieille cure	A fine green-colored French liqueur flavored with herbs and other ingredients.
vinaigretta	Vinaigrette. A cold salad dressing made with oil and vinegar, and seasoned with spices and chopped herbs.
vindaloo	Indian. A curried dish made with meat or shellfish, garlic, and wine or vinegar.
vichyssoise	A basic French soup made of leeks or scallions, onions, potatoes, chicken stock, milk and white pepper. Served chilled and garnished with chives.
vodka	Russian. A spirit distilled from rye, wheat, or potatoes with a bit of malt. Vodka is colorless, is not aged, and should be served cold.
vol-au-vent	A French puff pastry shell filled with small pieces of cooked meat, poultry or shellfish in a thick sauce.
Volcano	A bar drink made with Royal Chambord, Curaçao, and Champagne. Served in a champagne flute and garnished with a floating orange peel.
Voo Doo Juice	A bar drink made with a combination of orange, banana, coconut, and pineapple rums. Added to a mixture of orange, pineapple, and cranberry juices. Float dark rum on top and serve over ice in a hurricane glass.

Notes:
_____
_____
_____
_____
_____
_____
_____
_____
_____
_____

wafer	A small, thin, crisp cookie, cake, cracker, or candy.
walnut	The nut of a walnut tree. Walnuts have a buff, somewhat round, wrinkly shell with a beige, two-piece wrinkled kernel.

wareniki	Russian. A ravioli made of pasta stuffed with meat, cottage cheese, and cabbage. Served with melted butter.
wasabi	The green pungent root of an Asian herb (similar to horseradish) that is ground and used as a condiment. Wasabi is bottled and sold as a hot sauce.
water bath	*Bain marie.* A large pan of simmering water that is placed underneath the pan of food to be cooked. It is used to cook at a temperature just below the boiling point. This process may be done in the oven or on the stove top in a double boiler. ✓ A water bath is used in the preparation of sauces, creams, and foods that tend to curdle or stick to the pan if cooked over direct heat. ✓ Keep sauces and other delicate dishes at less than simmering heat. ✓ The microwave, if set for short amounts of time and watched closely, works just as well.
water chestnut	A crisp, white vegetable used especially in Chinese cuisine. It is the peeled root of an Asian marsh grass.
watercress	A pungent water plant that is used fresh as an herb and in salads.
watermelon	A large, oblong melon of African origin with a dark green, smooth rind that is sometimes striped. The flesh is sweet, succulent and red, orange or yellow. May be seedless or contain many black seeds.
Wiener	Short for wienerwurst. See frankfurter.
weiner krapfen	Austrian doughnuts made with a rich fermented dough.
Welsh rarebit	Welsh Rabbit. A snack made by pouring seasoned, melted cheese over toast or crackers.
whey	The watery part of milk after it has been separated from the curd during cheese making.
whip	To beat by hand, with mixer or blender, until fluffy.
whipped topping	❖ Canned whipping cream, which is kept in the refrigerated section, contains emulsifiers, stabilizers, cream, sugar, and nitrous oxide (laughing gas). It is expanded into a fluffy cream by the gas. ❖ A non-dairy whipped topping, which is kept in the refrigerated section and is made with hydrogenated vegetable oils. It contains no cream.
whipping cream	❖ Cream that contains 30-36% milk fat and that doubles in volume when whipped. Sometimes contains stabilizers and emulsifiers.
whisk	To beat fast in a circular motion so that a mixture is made lighter by incorporating air into it. This can be done with an electric mixer on high speed, a rotary beater, or by hand with a wire whisk.

whiskey	Whisky (Irish or Canadian). A spirit distilled from grain. The flavor and quality depends on the type of grain used, water source, number of distillations, the time aged, and the kind of barrels used. Scotch and Irish whiskies are made from barley. American and Canadian whiskies contain some barley malt, but Scotch and Irish whiskies have as much as 40% barley malt.
Whiskey Sour	A short bar drink made with blended whiskey, fresh lemon juice, and powdered sugar. Garnished with half a lemon slice and a maraschino cherry.
whitefish	A freshwater food fish with white flesh found in the Great Lakes of North America and other cold, fresh water lakes in Northern Europe and France.
whiting	A saltwater food fish found mainly in the north Atlantic.
White Russian	A bar drink made with vodka and Kahlúa over ice. Fill with light cream.
Wild Turkey	A Kentucky straight bourbon whisky originally produced by the Austin, Nichols Distilling Company in Lawrenceburg, Kentucky for the wealthy New York businessmen who attended the annual turkey hunt in North Carolina. It is carefully aged in charred oak barrels for eight years and sold at 101 proof and 86.8 proof.
windbeutel	German. A cream puff.
wine	A beverage made of the fermented juice of fresh grapes.
wine cooler	An alcoholic beverage made with a mixture of wine and a carbonated beverage. Served cold or over ice.
wine glass	A stemmed glass for drinking wine.
wine taster	❖ A person, usually a professional, who tastes and critiques wine. ❖ A small glass used for wine tasting.
winter greens	See kale.
witloof	See French endive.
wok	Chinese. A large bowl-shaped steel pan, usually fourteen inches in diameter, that is used for stir-frying, deep-frying, or steaming.
woodcock	Bécasse (French). Schnepfe (German). A woodland game bird used for food. Those native to the U.S. are smaller than the European species.
wood sorrel	A variety of herbs with acid sap.
won ton	Cantonese. Pockets of very thin noodle dough filled with meat or fish and vegetables, then boiled in soup or deep fried.

Worcestershire	A pungent savory sauce made with vinegar, soy sauce, and garlic. Used in making meat dishes.

Notes:

_____
_____
_____
_____
_____
_____
_____
_____
_____
_____
_____

X Y Z

yahni	A thick cut from a leg of mutton, with the bone, browned with onions and seasonings. Moistened in water and stewed in a covered dish in the oven.
yam	Portuguese. Spanish. An orange-fleshed sweet potato native to Africa that is used as a staple food.
yambalaya	Hindu. Diced raw ham sautéed in butter with chopped shallots, and red and green peppers that is simmered until done. Mixed with roast chicken that has been cubed and served together with rice pilaf.
yeast	A fungus that is used as a leavening agent. Yeast produces fermentation in dough which causes it to rise.
yeen-waw	Chinese. Bird's nest soup. See bird's nest soup.
yerba	Spanish meaning herb. ❖ A South American herb tea.
yogurt	A soft food made of fermented milk and milk solids with added cultures of beneficial bacteria. Can be plain or flavored.
Yorkshire pudding	A batter made of beaten eggs, flour, milk and salt that is poured into a skillet with beef drippings and baked. It is cut into squares and served with roast beef.
yu-chee	An Asian sauce made with chicken stock, ham, rice wine, and soy sauce. Usually served over beef or poultry.
Yukon Jack	A Canadian liquor that is 100 proof Canadian whiskey combined with a honey based liqueur.
yung-cheng	An Asian sauce made with sesame oil, white wine, ginger root, scallions, and salt.

zabaglione	A whipped topping made with egg yolks, sugar, and Marsala wine. Usually served over fruit.
zamponi di modena	Italian. Stuffed pig's foot. Boned pig's foot stuffed with forcemeat made of pork, green bacon, truffles, and seasoning. Cured, smoked, boiled and served with lentils.
zephir	A very light mousseline forcemeat made of fish, crustaceans, poultry, and stiffly beaten egg whites. Baked in a small dish and served as a hot appetizer.
zest	*Zeste* (French). The finely peeled or grated rind (outside skin) of citrus fruits such as lemons, limes, and oranges.
zester	A grater that removes the zest from citrus fruits.
zinfandel	❖ A small black grape. ❖ The dry red or white claret-type table wine that is made from the zinfandel grape that is grown mainly in California.
Zinger	A bar drink made with peach schnapps and Surge (a highly caffeinated citrus soda made by the Coca-Cola company).
Zombie	A tall bar drink made with light rum, créme de almond, sour mix, triple sec, orange juice, and 151 proof rum floated on top. Garnished with a maraschino cherry.
zucchetti	A small marrow.
zucchini	A long, cylindrical summer squash with smooth, dark green skin.
zuger kirschtorte	A dessert made with sponge cake soaked in a kirsch syrup, topped with butter cream and meringue, then garnished on the top and sides with toasted almond slivers.

Notes:

Abbreviations & Symbols:

i.e. (*id est*) that is   e.g. (*exempli gratia*) for example

et al (*et alia*) and others   etc. (*et cetera*) and so forth

❖   category marker   ✓ note or explanation

✎   basic ingredients or recipe

Notes:

Medical Terms

Medical Warning:

The medicinal values of herbs and spices are longstanding and well documented but are not, however, approved by the Federal Drug Administration. Please consult your doctor before use.

These supplements are not intended to replace modern medicine nor are they intended to diagnose, treat, cure, or prevent any disease. Keep in mind that, because these supplements have been and still are used as medicines, they contain chemicals that can be potentially harmful to certain individuals.

People with serious health problems should never attempt to replace their regular medications with herbal supplements unless directed to do so by their physician. Women who are pregnant or nursing should avoid taking herbal supplements, just as they would avoid alcohol and certain drugs, unless given express permission from their physician.

Anyone considering herbal supplements should consult a doctor of alternative medicine and be well informed before starting an herbal regimen. There is also a wide selection of literature available on natural medicine and herbal supplements at your local library, on the Internet, and in bookstores.

ajuvant	Assists in the prevention and cure of disease. Enhances the immune system.
anodyne	A substance that relieves pain. Sometimes has sedative qualities.
anthelmintic	Ability to expel or destroy parasitic worms, especially of the intestines.
anti-emetic	Reduces or prevents vomiting.
antipyretic	A substance that decreases fevers. Febrifuge.
antispasmodic	Works to prevent or relieve spasms or convulsions.
carminative	Expels gas from the alimentary canal in order to relieve colic or griping.
catarrhal	Decreases the inflammation in the mucous membranes of the nose and air passages.
cholagogue	A purgative that boosts liver function, stimulates the release of bile (gall) into the stomach, and improves digestion.
cholesterol	Cholesterol is a fat-like substance, lipid, that is naturally produced in the liver and helps with important body functions. ✓ High density lipids (HDL) or "good cholesterol" is high in protein and low in cholesterol. These lipids are believed to remove cholesterol from the blood reducing the risk of heart disease. ✓ Low density lipids (LDL) or "bad cholesterol" is high in cholesterol and low in protein. These lipids can accumulate on the walls of blood vessels and cause the formation of plaque (atherosclerosis or thickening of the arteries) which can lead to heart disease.

compress	Hot or cold application to the body. Dry - A dry cloth or towel containing either a hot or ice pack. Wet - A cloth or towel soaked in hot or cold water or in a medicinal solution.
counterirritant	Creates irritation in one place in order to reduce or counteract inflammation in another area.
decoction	The extract made by boiling an herb or spice down to a concentrate.
diaphoretic	Works to artificially increase or produce profuse perspiration. Sudorific.
discutient	A medicine that breaks up tumors.
diuretic	Increases the flow of urine.
emetic	Induces vomiting.
emmenagogue	A substance that stimulates menstrual flow.
expectorant	An agent that promotes the discharge or expulsion of mucus from the respiratory tract.
extract	A concentrate that is produced by extracting the active ingredients or medicinal compounds from an herb by using alcohol as a solvent.
farinaceous	Starchy or rich in starch.
infusion	Boiling water is poured over the leaves or flowers of an herb and allowed to steep, covered, for ten minutes.
laxative	A substance that relaxes or loosens the bowel in order to relieve constipation.
mucilaginous	A slimy plant substance or gum from plants such as seaweed that contains protein and sugars.
plaster	A medicinal dressing made of a piece of cloth or gauze that has been spread with a medicinal substance.
poultice	A soft, usually heated, and sometimes medicated mass spread on cloth and applied to sores or other lesions.
pungent	Stimulating to the mind and the senses.
resolvent	A preparation that reduces or eliminates a swelling.
restorative	A substance that reestablishes general health or vigor.
rubefacient	External application that produces redness of the skin.

sialagogue	Promotes the flow of saliva. Relieves dry mouth.
sudorific	Produces or promotes perspiration.
tea	A beverage made by steeping one teaspoon of herb in one cup of water. The ratio may vary depending on the strength of the herb.
tincture	A medicinal alcoholic extract made by combining a powdered herb in a 50% solution of alcohol.
tonic	An agent that increases body tone. One that invigorates, restores, refreshes, or stimulates. Increasing or restoring healthy physical or mental tone.
UTI	A urinary tract infection.

Notes: